WHAT'S WRONG
WITH A FREE LUNCH?

"*New Democracy Forum operates at a level of literacy and responsibility which is all too rare in our time.*" —John Kenneth Galbraith

Other books in the NEW DEMOCRACY FORUM series:

WHAT'S WRONG WITH A FREE LUNCH?

PHILIPPE VAN PARIJS

FOREWORD BY ROBERT M. SOLOW

EDITED BY JOSHUA COHEN AND JOEL ROGERS
FOR *BOSTON REVIEW*

BEACON PRESS
BOSTON

BEACON PRESS
25 Beacon Street
Boston, Massachusetts 02108-2892
www.beacon.org

Beacon Press books
are published under the auspices of
the Unitarian Universalist Association of Congregations.

Printed in the United States of America

05 04 03 02 01   8 7 6 5 4 3 2 1

Composition by Wilsted & Taylor Publishing Services

Library of Congress Cataloging-in-Publication Data
    What's wrong with a free lunch? / Philippe Van Parijs ; foreword by Robert
    M. Solow ; edited by Joshua Cohen and Joel Rogers for Boston Review.
        p.   cm.
    Includes bibliographical references and index.
        ISBN 0-8070-4713-9 (alk. paper)
      1. Income distribution. 2. Income maintenance programs. 3. Welfare
    economics. I. Parijs, Philippe Van, 1951– II. Cohen, Joshua, 1951–
    III. Rogers, Joel, 1952– IV. Boston review (Cambridge, Mass. : 1982)
        HC79.I5 W49   2001
        363.5'82—dc21

                                                    00-012254

CONTENTS

3

FOREWORD

ROBERT M. SOLOW

Imagine that someone proposes a radical innovation in social policy, in the case under consideration in this volume, the provision of a Universal Basic Income (UBI). The precise suggestion is that the government should pay a fixed monthly amount, the same for everyone, to each citizen (or resident) aged sixteen (for example) or older. This payment is not to be conditional on any behavior or characteristic of the recipient, other than being defined as an eligible member of the society.

The lively debate that follows explores the merits of this proposal. Philippe Van Parijs argues that a UBI, fixed at a subsistence level, would promote justice by increasing freedom, improve women's lives, and help the environment. In spite of the long history of resistance to redistributive social policy in the United States, I believe Van Parijs's proposal warrants serious discussion. But given its departure from prevailing attitudes about work and compensation (it breaks the link between reward and work) and its substantial cost, how shall we begin to think about the UBI?

One traditional way to sort things out is to divide the question into two parts. Is a UBI desirable? And is it feasible; can it be done? It may not be possible to make such a neat separation between desirability and feasibility. For instance, we might conclude after study that, yes, it can be done, but with certain side effects as consequences. We might then further conclude that those side effects tip the balance against the UBI, although the general idea seems quite acceptable, even advantageous.

The scenario might go like this: the availability of a UBI would lead some people to withdraw from the labor force because, with basic needs taken care of, they prefer a life of leisure to the combination of UBI plus wages plus the irksomeness of a job. The side effect of UBI is a somewhat lower income per head for the whole population, perhaps enough to control the decision. I emphasize that this is a made-up scenario, not a forecast. Protagonists of UBI might argue that, on the contrary, the availability of UBI would actually induce a net influx into the labor force, because the consequences of landing a bad job and failing at it would be less disastrous, and the normal human inclination to be active would take over. Belief that one of these outcomes is more likely than the other would have to come from the usual combination of a theory of labor-force participation and an appeal to data. My purpose was only to illustrate how the normative and the positive, though conceptually separate, may be closely intertwined.

Even with this possibility in mind, I think it is worthwhile to think first about the abstract desirability of a UBI. Someone who finds the idea unappealing in principle is not going to be moved by subtle econometrics. Two quite different lines of argument are proposed by those contributors who favor a UBI. Van Parijs himself, and some of his commentators, take a left-libertarian stance. The fundamental goal for social arrangements should be what they call "real" freedom. People should have not only the abstract right to choose the lifestyle that suits them but also the economic wherewithal to convert that right into lived reality. A UBI fixed at somewhere near subsistence opens such options as leisure, contemplation, study, unpopular artistic endeavor, or unpaid or poorly paid devotion to good works and good causes.

Some respondents who favor a UBI find this particular justification for it unattractive. Indeed left-libertarians seems to share with right-libertarians a view of a society as nothing but a collection of more or less isolated individuals, atoms. There is no trace of society as a cooperative enterprise, made possible by a preexisting web of fellow-feeling and mutual obligation. (In the libertarian view, cooperation can occur only when it is individually, even strategically, advantageous to each purely self-regarding participant.) As Edmund Phelps points out, the libertarian view creates a problem for the definition of eligibility for UBI; if just happening to be there is the criterion for membership, a hypothetical newly discovered population of Martians has a valid claim to a monthly check.

Other respondents offer a quite different justification for the institution of a UBI. It comes in two parts, a stock part and a flow part. On the stock side, the land and natural resources within any society's territory are seen as the patrimony of the entire group. A UBI—equal for all and unconditional—is one valid way of sharing this gift of nature, to which everyone has an equal claim; the income produced by natural capital can be seen as the economic base for a social dividend. (Of course this was one important basis for Henry George's advocacy of a land-value tax. It is a thought that might have appealed to the nations of the former Soviet Union, and might still appeal to developing countries.) The flow part starts from the observation that the annual production of a national economy must be owing in large part to social interactions, shared understandings, institutional capital—there are perhaps too many names for this—and not wholly to the efforts of individuals and their property. That common part is validly available for common purposes, and a UBI is at least one natural way to use it.

Some of the same commentators, and some others, find fault with the concept of UBI from a slightly different, but related, angle. They find the passive receipt of such a subsidy repugnant, and they think that this feeling is widely shared. Taking without giving violates a norm of reciprocity; the monthly check should be earned by some kind of service to society, even if not by paid employment. This is another way in which desirability and feasibility resist any clean separation: the thought is that this feature of the proposal is likely to make a UBI politically unacceptable.

This part of the discussion raises important questions about the design of redistributive policies even before issues of affordability are considered. Redistribution always creates losers as well as gainers, more or less by definition. (Van Parijs may be right that UBI will bring some efficiency gains via the mitigation of uncertainty, but he does not claim that these would be enough to cover the cost.) Anyone seeking democratic enactment of such a zero-sum policy urgently needs a broad consensus. Proponents of a UBI have something to learn from the reactions of fundamentally rather sympathetic commentators like those in this volume.

When I mentioned the issue of feasibility at the very beginning, I was thinking of economic, not political, viability. It is time to get back to that now. Obviously a very low-level UBI would be feasible in economic, even budgetary, terms, especially because it would at least partially replace some current means-tested transfers. Equally obviously, the immediate first-order gross cost of a meaningful UBI is one reality check. Van Parijs mentions a figure of $150 per person per month as a starting figure. There are about 210 million people aged 16 and older in the United States now, so the gross cost of this scheme would be about $380 billion a year. (The net cost would of course be less, depending on how other entitlements were affected.)

What should this figure be compared with? It is only about 3.5 percent of GDP, about the same as military spending. But that is about 18 percent of total federal (on-budget and off-budget) revenues, and therefore a major use of central government funds. Remember that this buys a UBI of $1,800 a year for a single person, probably not enough to buy a lot of "real" freedom. A larger UBI would have a proportionally higher gross cost. When you get to figures like $8,000 a year, approximately the "poverty line" for a single person, the gross cost is up to 16 percent of GDP and 80 percent of federal revenues. These are much more than marginal changes.

Ronald Dore speaks of spending 40 percent of GDP on a social dividend, roughly twice the current federal budget. But he is envisioning a society quite different from the one we have now. In Europe, the standard rule of thumb describes anything below half the median income as a degree of poverty that needs to be remedied. This has real advantages over the standard U.S. poverty line, which is known to be full of distortions, some up and some down, and anyway ignores the social and psychological importance of relative deprivation. The current median family income in the United States is about $40,000; so application of the European standard to a family with two adults would imply a UBI of $10,000. But it is not clear that the fundamental purpose of a UBI is the relief of poverty, however that is defined.

Anyway, this kind of easy calculation is not the fundamental one. Any nontrivial UBI will change the incentives faced by many people, indeed practically everyone: recipients of UBI checks, their relatives, taxpayers, employers, mortgage lenders, sellers of art supplies, you name it. When incentives change, behavior changes. In principle, you would want to know these "general equilibrium" effects of a UBI before deciding what you think about the proposal itself.

No one could actually carry out the complete calculation. Fortunately only some of the ramifications are likely to be important enough to matter, and those could perhaps be traced. For example, labor-supply effects are clearly of interest. If the institution of a UBI at some significant level were to induce many people to work less or not at all, then the aggregate income of the society would be lower and the fraction of it diverted to redistribution would be larger. Some respondents note that the supply of labor does not appear to be very sensitive to (small) changes in after-tax wage rates. That is fair comment. But UBI would involve both a higher tax rate and a lump-sum benefit; this combination of what economists call a substitution effect and an income effect would need to be analyzed carefully.

Earlier proposals for a negative income tax foundered on the realization that three desired outcomes of the NIT were arithmetically incompatible. The three were (a) that the system should provide a reasonable income for those without other income, (b) that it should not transfer any income to the well-off, and (c) that the marginal tax rate on low-wage earnings should not be discouragingly high. The UBI resolves this problem in a drastic way: it leaves the marginal tax rate on earnings exactly where it was before, but it transfers the same amount to rich and poor, thus roundly violating (b). So one cannot infer from the NIT history that the same adverse labor-supply effects would apply to UBI. But UBI offers problems of its own, and research and wider discussion will be needed to settle them.

That discussion is worth pursuing. Van Parijs and his respondents debate fundamental questions about the goals of social arrangements and how social policy can help create the kind of society we want to live in—about how to correct for poverty amidst plenty, and how to ensure that everyone gets a fair share of the benefits of social cooperation. While the market for redistributive social policy in the United States today remains limited, public debate about these important questions should be kept alive. This volume is a refreshing opening to that discussion.

EDITORS' PREFACE

JOSHUA COHEN AND JOEL ROGERS

In our statement of purpose for the New Democracy Forum (NDF), we promised politically engaged, intellectually honest, and morally serious debate about fundamental political issues, with an emphasis on constructive remedies. Achieving greater equality, we also said, would be a theme of many of NDF's discussions.

This NDF volume delivers squarely on that promise. The lead author, Philippe Van Parijs, is a Belgian political theorist and prominent proponent of a Universal Basic Income (UBI) policy. Under a UBI scheme, all adult members of society would be guaranteed a basic income. Everyone: dotcommers and waitress moms, doctors and ski bums. And unconditionally: UBI would not require one to work, or engage in other socially constructive activity. Van Parijs recommends UBI in part on practical grounds: he thinks it would ease labor market problems, both of the American (low-wage) and Western European (high-unemployment) kind. But his principal argument is about *freedom*. Guarantee everyone a basic income, and they will be in a better position to pursue their aspirations, refuse grueling work, and exit from abusive relationships. In short, UBI means more *real* freedom, for all.

{ xvii }

Some of the respondents to Van Parijs are supporters, who present further arguments for UBI and strategies for achieving it in the real world of American politics. Others are friendly critics, who quarrel about the proper size of a UBI, and the best way to finance it. And some are opponents, who reject UBI on the grounds that it conflicts with the value of reciprocity: people who work hard are entitled to a fair return, but people are not entitled to basic income just because they live in the United States.

These normative arguments aside, UBI proposals are commonly assailed as simply too costly. And here what is striking is that no party to this discussion condemns UBI on grounds of cost (William Galston reports a "suspicion" about costs, but focuses his criticism elsewhere). The main hurdles to establishing a UBI in the United States are honest disagreements of political morality and depressing failures of political imagination. UBI could be done. The question is whether we want to achieve it.

1

A BASIC INCOME FOR ALL

Entering the new millennium, I submit for discussion a proposal for the improvement of the human condition: namely,
that everyone should be paid a *universal basic income* (UBI),
at a level *sufficient for subsistence.*

In a world in which a child under five dies of malnutrition
every two seconds, and close to a third of the planet's population lives in a state of "extreme poverty" that often proves
fatal, the global enactment of such a basic income proposal
may seem wildly utopian. Readers may suspect it to be impossible even in the wealthiest of OECD nations.

Yet, in those nations, productivity, wealth, and national
incomes have advanced sufficiently far to support an adequate UBI. And if enacted, a basic income would serve as a
powerful instrument of social justice: it would promote real
freedom for all by providing the material resources that people need to pursue their aims. At the same time, it would
help to solve the policy dilemmas of poverty and unemployment, and serve ideals associated with both the feminist and
green movements. So I will argue.

I am convinced, along with many others in Europe, that—
far from being utopian—a UBI makes common sense in the

current context of the European Union.[1] As Brazilian senator Eduardo Suplicy has argued, it is also relevant to less-developed countries—not only because it helps keep alive the remote promise of a high level of social solidarity without the perversity of high unemployment, but also because it can inspire and guide more modest immediate reforms.[2] And if a UBI makes sense in Europe and in less developed countries, why should it not make equally good (or perhaps better) sense in North America?[3] After all, the United States is the only country in the world in which a UBI is already in place: in 1999, the Alaska Permanent Fund paid each person of whatever age who had been living in Alaska for at least one year an annual UBI of $1,680. This payment admittedly falls far short of subsistence, but it has nonetheless become far from negligible two decades after its inception. Moreover, there was a public debate about UBI in the United States long before it started in Europe. In 1967, Nobel economist James Tobin published the first technical article on the subject, and a few years later, he convinced George McGovern to promote a UBI, then called "demogrant," in his 1972 presidential campaign.[4]

To be sure, after this short public life the UBI sank into near-oblivion in North America. For good reasons? I believe not. There are many relevant differences between the United States and the European Union in terms of labor markets, educational systems, and ethnic makeup. But none of them makes the UBI intrinsically less appropriate for the United States than for the European Union. More important are the significant differences in the balance of political forces. In the United States, far more than in Europe, the political viability of a proposal is deeply affected by how much it caters to the tastes of wealthy campaign donors. This is bound to be a serious additional handicap for any proposal that aims to expand options for, and empower, the least wealthy. But let's not turn necessity into virtue, and sacrifice justice in the name of increased political feasibility. When fighting to reduce the impact of economic inequalities on the political agenda, it is essential, in the United States as elsewhere, to propose, explore, and advocate ideas that are ethically compelling and make economic sense, even when their political feasibility remains uncertain. Sobered, cautioned, and strengthened by Europe's debate of the last two decades, here is my modest contribution to this task.

UBI DEFINED

By *universal basic income* I mean an income paid by a government, at a uniform level and at regular intervals, to each adult member of society. The grant is paid, and its level is fixed, irrespective of whether the person is rich or poor, lives alone or with others, is willing to work or not. In most versions—certainly in mine—it is granted not only to citizens, but to all permanent residents.

The UBI is called "basic" because it is something on which a person can safely count, a material foundation on which a life can firmly rest. Any other income—whether in cash or in kind, from work or savings, from the market or the state—can lawfully be added to it. On the other hand, nothing in the definition of UBI, as it is here understood, connects it to some notion of "basic needs." A UBI, as defined, can fall short of or exceed what is regarded as necessary to a decent existence.

I favor the highest sustainable such income, and believe that all the richer countries can now afford to pay a basic income above subsistence. But advocates of a UBI do not need to press for a basic income at this level right away. In fact, the easiest and safest way forward, though details may differ considerably from one country to another, is likely to consist of enacting a UBI first at a level below subsistence, and then increasing it over time.

The idea of the UBI is at least a hundred and fifty years old. Its two earliest known formulations were inspired by Charles Fourier, the prolific French utopian socialist. In 1848, while Karl Marx was finishing off the Communist Manifesto around the corner, the Brussels-based Fourierist author Joseph Charlier published *Solution of the Social Problem*, in which he argued for a "territorial dividend" owed to each citizen by virtue of our equal ownership of the nation's territory. The following year, John Stuart Mill published a new edition of his *Principles of Political Economy*, which contains a sympathetic presentation of Fourierism ("the most skillfully combined, and with the greatest foresight of objections, of all the forms of Socialism") rephrased so as to yield an unambiguous UBI proposal: "In the distribution, a certain minimum is first assigned for the subsistence of every member of the community, whether capable or not of labour. The remainder of the produce is shared in certain proportions, to be determined beforehand, among the three elements, Labour, Capital, and Talent."[5]

Under various labels—"state bonus," "national dividend," "social dividend," "citizen's wage," "citizen's income," "universal grant," "basic income," etc.—the idea of a UBI was repeatedly taken up in intellectual circles throughout the twentieth century. It was seriously discussed by left-wing academics such as G. D. H. Cole and James Meade in England between the World Wars and, via Abba Lerner, it seems to have inspired Milton Friedman's proposal for a "negative income tax."[6] But only since the late 1970s has the idea gained real political currency in a number of European countries, starting with the Netherlands and Denmark. A number of political parties, usually green or "left-liberal" (in the European sense), have now made it part of their official party program.

UBI and Existing Programs

To appreciate the significance of this interest and support, it is important to understand how a UBI differs from existing benefit schemes. It obviously differs from traditional social-insurance based income-maintenance institutions (such as

Social Security), whose benefits are restricted to wage workers who have contributed enough out of their past earnings to become eligible. But it also differs from Western European or North American conditional minimum-income schemes (such as welfare).

Many, indeed most West European countries introduced some form of guaranteed minimum-income scheme at some point after World War II.[7] But these schemes remain conditional. To receive an income grant a beneficiary must meet more or less stringent variants of the following three requirements: if she is able to work, she must be willing to accept a suitable job, or to undergo suitable training, if offered; she must pass a means test, in the sense that she is only entitled to the benefit if there are grounds to believe that she has no access to a sufficient income from other sources; and her household situation must meet certain criteria—it matters, for example, whether she lives on her own, with a person who has a job, with a jobless person, etc. By contrast, a UBI does not require satisfaction of any of these conditions.

Advocates of a UBI may, but generally do not, propose it as a full substitute for existing conditional transfers. Most supporters want to keep—possibly in simplified forms and necessarily at reduced levels—publicly organized social insurance and disability compensation schemes that would supplement the unconditional income while remaining subject to the usual conditions. Indeed, if a government implemented an unconditional income that was too small to cover basic needs—which, as I previously noted, would almost certainly be the case at first—UBI advocates would not want to eliminate the existing conditional minimum-income schemes, but only to readjust their levels.

In the context of Europe's most developed welfare states, for example, one might imagine the immediate introduction of universal child benefits and a strictly individual, noncontributory basic pension as full substitutes for existing means-tested benefit schemes for the young and the elderly. Indeed, some of these countries already have such age-restricted UBIs for the young and the elderly. Contributory retirement insurance schemes, whether obligatory or optional, would top up the basic pension.

As for the working-age population, advocates of a universal minimum income could, in the short term, settle for a "partial" (less-than-subsistence) but strictly individual UBI, initially pitched at, say, half the current guaranteed minimum income for a single person. In U.S. terms, that would be about $250 per month, or $3,000 a year. For households whose net earnings are insufficient to reach the socially defined subsistence level, this unconditional and individual floor would be supplemented by means-tested benefits, differentiated according to household size and subjected, as they are now, to some work requirements.

UBI and Some Alternatives

While the UBI is different from traditional income maintenance schemes, it also differs from a number of other innovative proposals that have attracted recent attention. Perhaps closest to a UBI are various negative income tax (NIT) proposals.[8]

NIT

Though the details vary, the basic idea of a negative income tax is to grant each citizen a basic income, but in the form of a refundable tax credit. From the personal tax liability of each household, one subtracts the sum of the basic incomes of its members. If the difference is positive, a tax needs to be paid. If it is negative, a benefit (or negative tax) is paid by the government to the household. In principle, one can achieve exactly the same distribution of post-tax-and-transfer income among households with a UBI or with an NIT. Indeed, the NIT might be cheaper to run, since it avoids the to-and-fro that results from paying a basic income to those with a substantial income and then taxing it back.

Still, a UBI has three major advantages over an NIT. First, any NIT scheme would have the desired effects on poverty only if it was supplemented by a system of advance payments sufficient to keep people from starving before their tax forms are examined at the end of the fiscal year. But from what we know of social welfare programs, ignorance or confusion is bound to prevent some people from getting access to such advance payments. The higher rate of take-up that is bound to be associated with a UBI scheme matters greatly to anyone who wants to fight poverty.

Second, although an NIT could in principle be individualized, it operates most naturally and is usually proposed at the household level. As a result, even if the inter-household distribution of income were exactly the same under an NIT and the corresponding UBI, the intra-household distribution will be far less unequal under the UBI. In particular, under current circumstances, the income that directly accrues to women will be considerably higher under the UBI than the NIT, since the latter tends to ascribe to the household's higher earner at least part of the tax credit of the low- or non-earning partner.

Third, a UBI can be expected to deal far better than an NIT with an important aspect of the "unemployment trap" that is stressed by social workers but generally overlooked by economists. Whether it makes any sense for an unemployed person to look for or accept a job does not depend only on the difference between income at work and out of work. What deters people from getting out to work is often a reasonable fear of uncertainty. While they try a new job, or just after they lose one, the regular flow of benefits is often interrupted. The risk of administrative time lags—especially among people who may have a limited knowledge of their entitlements and the fear of going into debt, or for people who are likely to have no savings to fall back on—may make sticking to benefits the wisest option. Unlike an NIT, a UBI provides a firm basis of income that keeps flowing whether one is in or out of work. And it is therefore far better suited to handle this aspect of the poverty trap.

The Stakeholder Society

UBI also differs from the lump-sum grant, or "stake," that Thomas Paine and Orestes Brownson—and, more recently, Bruce Ackerman and Anne Alstott—have suggested be universally awarded to citizens at their maturity in a refashioned "stakeholder society."[9] Ackerman and Alstott propose that, upon reaching age twenty-one, every citizen, rich or poor, should be awarded a lump-sum stake of $80,000. This money can be used in any way its recipient wishes—from investing in the stock market or paying for college fees to blowing it all in a wild night of gambling. The stake is not conditioned on recipients being "deserving," or having shown any interest in contributing to society. Funding would be provided by a 2 percent wealth tax, which could be gradually replaced over time (assuming a fair proportion of recipients ended their lives with enough assets) by a lump-sum estate tax of $80,000 (in effect requiring the recipient to pay back the stake).

I am not opposed to a wealth or estate tax, nor do I think it is a bad idea to give everyone a little stake to get going with their adult life. Moreover, giving a large stake at the beginning of adult life might be regarded as formally equivalent—with some freedom added—to giving an equivalent amount as a life-long unconditional income. After all, if the stake is assumed to be paid back at the end of a person's life, as it is in the Ackerman and Alstott proposal, the equivalent annual amount is simply the stake multiplied by the real rate of interest, say an amount in the (very modest) order of $2,000 annually, or hardly more than Alaska's dividend. If instead people are entitled to consume their stake through life—and who would stop them?—the equivalent annual income would be significantly higher.

Whatever the level, given the choice between an initial endowment and an equivalent lifelong UBI, we should go for the latter. Endowments are rife with opportunities for waste, especially among those less well equipped by birth and background to make use of the opportunity the stake supplies. To achieve, on an ongoing basis, the goal of some baseline income maintenance, it would therefore be necessary to keep a means-tested welfare system, and we would be essentially back to our starting point—the need and desirability of a UBI as an alternative to current provisions.

WHY A UBI?

So much for definitions and distinctions. Let us now turn to the central case for a UBI.

Justice

The main argument for UBI is founded on a view of justice. Social justice, I believe, requires that our institutions be designed to best secure *real freedom* to all.[10] Such a real-libertarian conception of justice combines two ideas. First, the members of society should be formally free, with a well-enforced structure of property rights and personal liberties. What matters to a real libertarian, however, is not only the protection of individual rights, but assurances of the real value of those rights: we need to be concerned not only with liberty, but, in John Rawls's phrase, with the "worth of liberty." At first approximation, the worth or real value of a person's liberty depends on the resources the person has at her command to make use of her liberty. So it is therefore necessary that the distribution of opportunity—understood as access to the means that people need for doing what they might want to do—be designed to offer the greatest possible real opportunity to those with fewest opportunities, subject to everyone's formal freedom being respected.

This notion of a just, free society needs to be specified and clarified in many respects.[11] But in the eyes of anyone who finds it attractive, there cannot but be a strong presumption in favor of UBI. A cash grant to all, no questions asked, no strings attached, at the highest sustainable level, can hardly fail to advance that ideal. Or if it does not, the burden of argument lies squarely on the side of the challengers.

Jobs and Growth

A second way to make the case for UBI is more policy-oriented. A UBI might be seen as a way to solve the apparent dilemma between a European-style combination of limited poverty and high unemployment and an American-style combination of low unemployment and widespread poverty. The argument can be spelled out schematically as follows.

For over two decades, most Western European countries have been experiencing massive unemployment. Even at the peak of the jobs cycle, millions of Europeans are vainly seeking work. How can this problem be tackled? For a while, the received wisdom was to deal with massive unemployment by speeding up the rate of growth. But considering the speed with which technological progress was eliminating jobs, it became apparent that a fantastic rate of growth would be necessary even to keep employment stable, let alone reduce the number of unemployed. For environmental and other reasons, such a rate of growth would not be desirable. An alternative strategy was to consider a substantial reduction in workers' earnings. By reducing the relative cost of labor, technology could be redirected in such a way that fewer jobs were sacrificed. A more modest and therefore sustainable growth rate might then be able to stabilize and gradually reduce present levels of unemployment. But this could only be achieved at the cost of imposing an unacceptable standard of living on a large part of the population, all the more unacceptable because a reduction in wages would require a parallel reduction in unemployment benefits and other replacement incomes, so as to preserve work incentives.

If we reject both accelerated growth and reduced earnings, must we also give up on full employment? Yes, if by full employment we mean a situation in which virtually everyone who wants a *full-time* job can obtain one that is both affordable for the employer *without any subsidy* and affordable for the worker *without any additional benefit*. But perhaps not, if we are willing to redefine full employment by either shortening the working week, paying subsidies to employers, or paying subsidies to employees.

A first option, particularly fashionable in France at the moment, consists in a social redefinition of "full time"—that is, a reduction in maximum working time, typically in the form of a reduction in the standard length of the working week. The underlying idea is to ration jobs: because there are not enough jobs for everyone who would like one, let us not allow a subset to appropriate them all.

On closer scrutiny, however, this strategy is less helpful than it might seem. If the aim is to reduce unemployment, the reduction in the work week must be dramatic enough to more than offset the rate of productivity growth. If this dramatic reduction is matched by a proportional fall in earnings, the lowest wages will then fall—unacceptably—below the social minimum. If, instead, total earnings are maintained at the same level, if only for the less well paid, labor costs will rise. The effect on unemployment will then be reduced, if not reversed, as the pressure to eliminate the less skilled jobs through mechanization is stepped up. In other words, a dramatic reduction in working time looks bound to be detrimental to the least qualified jobs—either because it kills the supply (they pay less than replacement incomes) or because it kills the demand (they cost firms a lot more per hour than they used to).

It does not follow that the reduction of the standard working week can play no role in a strategy for reducing unemployment without increasing poverty. But to avoid the dilemma thus sketched, it needs to be coupled with explicit or implicit subsidies to low-paid jobs. For example, a reduction of the standard working week did play a role in the so-called "Dutch miracle"—the fact that, in the last decade or so, jobs expanded much faster in the Netherlands than elsewhere in Europe. But this was mainly as a result of the standard working week falling below firms' usual operating time and thereby triggering a restructuring of work organization that involved far more part-time jobs. But these jobs could not have developed without the large implicit subsidies they enjoy, in the Netherlands, by virtue of a universal basic pension, universal child benefits, and a universal health care system.

Any strategy for reducing unemployment without increasing poverty depends, then, on some variety of the *active* welfare state—that is, a welfare state that does not subsidize passivity (the unemployed, the retired, the disabled, etc.) but systematically and permanently (if modestly) subsidizes productive activities. Such subsidies can take many different forms. At one extreme they can take the form of general subsidies to employers at a level that is gradually reduced as the hourly wage rate increases. Edmund Phelps has advocated a scheme of this sort, restricted to full-time workers, for the United States.[12] In Europe, this approach usually takes the form of proposals to abolish employers' social security contributions on the lower earnings while maintaining the workers' entitlements to the same level of benefits.

At the other extreme we find the UBI, which can also be understood as a subsidy, but one paid to the employee (or potential employee), thereby giving her the option of accepting a job with a lower hourly wage or with shorter hours than she otherwise could. In between, there are a large number of other schemes, such as the U.S. Earned Income Tax Credit and various benefit programs restricted to people actually working or actively looking for full-time work.

A general employment subsidy and a UBI are very similar in terms of the underlying economic analysis and, in part, in what they aim to achieve. For example, both address head-on the dilemma mentioned in connection with reductions in work time: they make it possible for the least skilled to be employed at a lower cost to their employer, without thereby impoverishing workers.

The two approaches are, however, fundamentally different in one respect. With employer subsidies, the pressure to take up employment is kept intact, possibly even increased; with a UBI, that pressure is reduced. This is not because permanent idleness becomes an attractive option: even a large UBI cannot be expected to secure a comfortable standard of living on its own. Instead, a UBI makes it easier to take a break between two jobs, reduce working time, make room for more training, take up self-employment, or join a cooperative. And with a UBI, workers will only take a job if they find it suitably attractive, while employer subsidies make unattractive, low-productivity jobs more economically viable. If the motive in combating unemployment is not some sort of work fetishism—an obsession with keeping everyone busy—but rather a concern to give every person the possibility of taking up gainful employment in which she can find recognition and accomplishment, then the UBI is to be preferred.

Feminist and Green Concerns

A third piece of the argument for a UBI takes particular note of its contribution to realizing the promise of the feminist and green movements. The contribution to the first should be obvious. Given the sexist division of labor in the household and the special "caring" functions that women disproportionately bear, their labor market participation, and range of choice in jobs, is far more constrained than

{ 19 }

those of men. Both in terms of direct impact on the inter-individual distribution of income and the longer-term impact on job options, a UBI is therefore bound to benefit women far more than men. Some of them, no doubt, will use the greater material freedom UBI provides to reduce their paid working time and thereby lighten the "double shift" at certain periods of their lives. But who can sincerely believe that working subject to the dictates of a boss for forty hours a week is a path to liberation? Moreover, it is not only against the tyranny of bosses that a UBI supplies some protection, but also against the tyranny of husbands and bureaucrats. It provides a modest but secure basis on which the more vulnerable can stand, as marriages collapse or administrative discretion is misused.

To discuss the connection between UBI and the green movement, it is useful to view the latter as an alliance of two components. Very schematically, the *environmental* component's central concern is with the *pollution* generated by industrial society. Its central objective is the establishment of a society that can be sustained by its physical environment. The *green-alternative* component's central concern, on the other hand, is with the *alienation* generated by industrial society. Its central objective is to establish a society in which people spend a great deal of their time on "autonomous" activities, ruled by neither the market nor the state. For both components, there is something very attractive in the idea of a UBI.

The environmentalists' chief foe is productivism, the obsessive pursuit of economic growth. And one of the most powerful justifications for fast growth, in particular among the working class and its organizations, is the fight against unemployment. The UBI, as argued above, is a coherent strategy for tackling unemployment without relying on faster growth. The availability of such a strategy undermines the broad productivist coalition and thereby improves the prospects for realizing environmentalist objectives in a world in which pollution (even in the widest sense) is not the only thing most people care about.

Green-alternatives should also be attracted to basic income proposals, for a UBI can be viewed as a general subsidy financed by the market and state spheres to the benefit of the autonomous sphere. This is in part because the UBI gives everyone some real freedom—as opposed to a sheer right—to withdraw from paid employment in order to perform autonomous activities, such as grass-roots militancy or unpaid care work. But part of the impact also consists in giving the least well endowed greater power to turn down jobs that they do not find sufficiently fulfilling, and thereby creating incentives to design and offer less alienated employment.

Some Objections

Suppose everything I have said thus far is persuasive: that the UBI, if it could be instituted, would be a natural and attractive way of ensuring a fair distribution of real freedom, fighting unemployment without increasing poverty, and promoting the central goals of both the feminist and the green movements. What are the objections?

Perhaps the most common is that a UBI would cost too much. Such a statement is of course meaningless if the amount and the scale is left unspecified. At a level of $150 per month and per person, a UBI is obviously affordable in some places, since this is the monthly equivalent of what every Alaskan receives as an annual dividend. Could one afford a UBI closer to the poverty line? By simply multiplying the poverty threshold for a one-person household by the population of a country, one soon reaches scary amounts—often well in excess of the current level of total government expenditure.

But these calculations are misleading. A wide range of existing benefits can be abolished or reduced once a UBI is in place. And for most people of working age, the basic income and the increased taxes (most likely in the form of an abolition of exemptions and of low tax rates for the lowest income brackets) required to pay for it will largely offset each other. In a country such as the United States, which has developed a reasonably effective revenue collection system, what matters is not the gross cost but its distributive impact—which could easily work out the same for a UBI or an NIT.

Estimates of the net budgetary cost of various UBI and NIT schemes have been made both in Europe and the United States.[13] Obviously, the more comprehensive and generous existing means-tested minimum-income schemes are, the more limited the net cost of a UBI scheme at a given level. But the net cost is also heavily affected by two other factors. Does the scheme aim to achieve an effective rate of taxation (and hence of disincentive to work) at the lower end of the distribution of earnings that is no higher than the tax rates higher up? And does it give the same amount to each member of a couple as to a single person? If the answer is positive on both counts, a scheme that purports to lift every household out of poverty has a very high net cost, and would therefore generate major shifts in the income distribution, not only from richer to poorer households, but also from single people to couples.[14] This does not mean that it is "unaffordable," but that a gradual approach is required if sudden sharp falls in the disposable incomes of some households are to be avoided. A basic income or negative income tax at the household level is one possible option. A strictly individual, but "partial" basic income, with means-tested income supplements for single adult households, is another.

A second frequent objection is that a UBI would have perverse labor supply effects. (In fact, some American income maintenance experiments in the 1970s showed such effects.) The first response should be: "So what?" Boosting the labor supply is no aim in itself. No one can reasonably want an overworked, hyperactive society. Give people of all classes the opportunity to reduce their working time or even take a complete break from work in order to look after their children or elderly relatives. You will not only save on prisons and hospitals. You will also improve the human capital of the next generation. A modest UBI is a simple and effective instrument in the service of keeping a socially and economically sound balance between the supply of paid labor and the rest of our lives.

It is of the greatest importance that our tax-and-transfer systems not trap the least skilled, or those whose options are limited for some other reason, in a situation of idleness and dependency. But it is precisely awareness of this risk that has been the most powerful factor in arousing public interest for a UBI in those European countries in which a substantial means-tested guaranteed minimum income had been operating for some time. It would be absurd to deny that such schemes depress in undesirable ways workers' willingness to accept low-paid jobs and stick with them, and therefore also employers' interest in designing and offering such jobs. But reducing the level or security of income support, on the pattern of the United States 1996 welfare reform, is not the only possible response. Reducing the various dimensions of the unemployment trap by turning means-tested schemes into universal ones is another. Between these two routes, there cannot be much doubt about what is to be preferred by people committed to combining a sound economy and a fair society—as opposed to boosting labor supply to the maximum.

A third objection is moral rather than simply pragmatic. A UBI, it is often said, gives the undeserving poor something for nothing. According to one version of this objection, a UBI conflicts with the fundamental principle of reciprocity: the idea that people who receive benefits should respond in kind by making contributions. Precisely because it is unconditional, it assigns benefits even to those who make no social contribution—who spend their mornings bickering with their partner, surf off Malibu in the afternoon, and smoke pot all night.

One might respond by simply asking how many would actually choose this life? How many, compared to the countless people who spend most of their days doing socially useful but unpaid work? Everything we know suggests that nearly all people seek to make some contribution. And many of us believe that it would be positively awful to try to turn all socially useful contributions into waged employment. On this background, even the principle "To each according to her contribution" justifies a modest UBI as part of its best feasible institutional implementation.

But a more fundamental reply is available. True, a UBI is undeserved good news for the idle surfer. But this good news is ethically indistinguishable from the undeserved luck that massively affects the present distribution of wealth, income, and leisure. Our race, gender, and citizenship, how educated and wealthy we are, how gifted in math and how fluent in English, how handsome and even how ambitious, are overwhelmingly a function of who our parents happened to be and of other equally arbitrary contingencies. Not even the most narcissistic self-made man could think that he fixed the parental dice in advance of entering this world. Such gifts of luck are unavoidable and, if they are fairly distributed, unobjectionable. A minimum condition for a fair distribution is that everyone should be guaranteed a modest share of these undeserved gifts.[15] Nothing could achieve this more securely than a UBI.

Such a moral argument will not be sufficient in reshaping the politically possible. But it may well prove crucial. Without needing to deny the importance of work and the role of personal responsibility, it will save us from being overimpressed by a fashionable political rhetoric that justifies bending the least advantaged more firmly under the yoke. It will make us even more confident about the rightness of a universal basic income than about the rightness of universal suffrage. It will make us even more comfortable about everyone being entitled to an income, even the lazy, than about everyone being entitled to a vote, even the incompetent.

2

WHAT ABOUT RECIPROCITY?

WILLIAM A. GALSTON

Philippe Van Parijs is to be congratulated for making a bold and challenging proposal. It is, in the literal sense of an overused phrase, thought provoking. It is not equally likely to provoke agreement, however, and I find myself unpersuaded. Everything that is morally and practically sound in the UBI can be achieved by other policies, and the ends that are peculiar to the UBI lack moral and practical force.

Setting aside my suspicion that a significant UBI would be unaffordable and would have labor-supply effects that even its advocates would deem perverse, here are my core objections to this proposal.

1. If implemented in some nations but not others (as it almost surely would be), the UBI could well spark an international crisis and devastating domestic backlash. Imagine, for example, that the United States adopted this idea but Mexico did not. The incentives to leave Mexico and enter the United States, already powerful, would intensify dramatically. At the same time, it would no longer be possible for those of us who favor a relatively open immigration policy to defend it by invoking the contributions that immigrants will make. Just imagine the political power of the counterarguments that Pat Buchanan (or, in the European

context, Le Pen and Haider) would make. One may restrict the UBI, as Van Parijs does, to permanent residents, but this will only increase the propensity of recipient nations to favor temporary workers over new permanent residents.

2. Van Parijs justifies the UBI in part as a way out of the unpleasant choice between Europe's low poverty and high unemployment, and America's low unemployment and widespread poverty. My counterargument is that the UBI is not needed to solve either of these problems. Europe's high unemployment is the predictable consequence of its rigid labor market policies, but greater flexibility need not impoverish European workers. In fact, many European nations have begun to adjust, and their rates of unemployment are declining, in many cases quite sharply. In the United States, a sustained tight labor market is lifting real wages for workers at the end of the queue, and, as Rebecca Blank has shown, the massive increase in the Earned Income Tax Credit enacted by the Clinton administration in 1993 significantly reduced the incidence of working poverty in the United States. Increases in the minimum wage have also helped, and many of us believe that it would be a good idea to index the minimum wage for inflation to eliminate the possibility of repeating past episodes of neglect that have eroded its real value.

3. I agree with Van Parijs that it would be desirable to bolster support for socially useful activities—such as caregiving and participating in public-spirited voluntary associations—that are not adequately included in the current wage sys-

tem. But this goal, too, can be promoted through policies other than the UBI. Since 1994, more than 100,000 Americans have had the opportunity through AmeriCorps to engage in compensated national and community service. I believe that this opportunity should be made available to everyone who wishes to serve. More recently, we have begun to use the tax code to compensate family members and others who find themselves spending substantial portions of their days caring for children or for aging or dependent relatives. These social supports can and should be broadened. But none of these strategies requires anything like a UBI.

4. Van Parijs's thesis advances, and to some extent rests upon, various animadversions concerning work. He invokes the familiar categories of meaninglessness and alienation; he denounces "work fetishism" and the spectre of an "overworked, hyperactive society." In the process, he systematically overlooks the positive dimensions of work. As William Julius Wilson has pointed out, work is an important way of organizing our lives, of giving structure and meaning to what can otherwise become a formless and purposeless existence. Work helps young people make the transition to psychological adulthood and in many cases serves as a source of economic and social mobility. It is also the case (some regard this as a sad fact, others as happy) that much of what we value comes into being as the result of work, and would not exist otherwise. As has been observed at least since the Bible, work has a negative dimension, an element of compulsion. But surveys indicate that, at least in the

United States, attitudes toward work are surprisingly positive. Perhaps Van Parijs's negative tone has more resonance in Europe.

5. My most fundamental objection to the UBI is moral. I incline toward the principle that Van Parijs downplays: reciprocity, the simple but profound idea that people who receive benefits should make contributions—if they are able. The qualification suffices to show why reciprocity cannot be a complete theory of social justice. But while reciprocity is not sufficient for such a theory, it is, I believe, necessary.

Van Parijs offers two responses, neither very compelling. The first is that even under a UBI most people would want to make a contribution, so that violations of reciprocity would be *de minimis*. I doubt it. But even if he is right about this, it is a claim that accepts reciprocity as a basis of moral justification. (In fairness, he is aware of this.)

Van Parijs's second response is that while the UBI is undeserved good news for the idle Malibu surfer, existing arrangements also massively reflect undeserved luck. While we can argue about who deserves what and about the extent of undeserved distributions in different societies, Van Parijs is surely right about this factual claim. But how does it follow morally that we should replace the current system of distribution with a UBI? One could say with equal (indeed greater) plausibility that we should search for mechanisms that better reflect the principle of contribution. And without getting mired in the theoretical details, I would point

out that while John Rawls also takes the critique of undeserved luck as a point of departure, he arrives at conclusions
very different from Van Parijs's. These differences, which
may owe in part to empirical assumptions (Van Parijs recognizes this), seem also to reflect a deeper normative disagreement. Rawls presents his conception of political community as a system of social cooperation, and he understands
social justice as the fair organization of such a cooperative
venture and fair allocation of its joint products. Despite my
many disagreements with Rawls, I think this point of departure is clearly preferable to Van Parijs's "real libertarianism," however sophisticated. To be sure, this bald statement
of differences between my approach to these matters and
that of Van Parijs doesn't settle anything, but I believe it
frames the disagreement in the right way.

UBI AND THE FLAT TAX

HERBERT A. SIMON

I am in strong general agreement with Philippe Van Parijs's argument for a UBI or "patrimony"—a portion of the product of a society that should be shared by all of those who inhabit that society. To establish such a patrimony is equivalent to recognizing shared ownership of a significant fraction of the resources, physical and intellectual, that enable the society to produce what it produces. As the essay makes a very strong case for the UBI and its feasibility, I will limit my comments to just two issues: (1) why a UBI (or patrimony) would be just; and (2) some problems of incentives that such a system poses and that need to be handled effectively.

JUSTICE

When we compare average incomes in rich nations with those in Third World countries, we find enormous differences that are surely not due simply to differences in motivations to earn. Laziness is not a principal cause of poverty. A more plausible explanation for the differences, in fact the explanation that is universally put forward, is that much greater resources per capita are available to some countries than to others. These differences are not simply a matter of acres of land or tons of coal or iron ore, but, more important, differences in social capital—principally, differences in stored knowledge (e.g., technology, and especially organizational and governmental skills).

Exactly the same claim can be made about the differences in incomes within any given society. In large part, these differences must be attributed to differences in capital ownership, of which the largest part is social capital: knowledge, and participation in kinship and other privileged social relations. In addressing the question of justice, therefore, we are assessing the justice of inheritance of such resources along bloodlines. This is a question of value, not of fact. I personally do not see any moral basis for an inalienable right to inherit resources, or to retain all the resources that one has acquired by means of economic or other activities.

The usual argument for such a right is based on the assumption of perfectly competitive markets where factors of production are paid their marginal values and where there are no externalities. But this assumption does not hold to any reasonable degree of approximation in real societies. Access to the social capital—a major source of differences in income, between and within societies—is in large part the product of externalities: membership in a particular society, and interaction with other members of that society under practices that commonly give preferred access to particular members.

How large are these externalities, which must be regarded as owned jointly by members of the whole society? When we compare the poorest with the richest nations, it is hard to conclude that social capital can produce less than about 90 percent of income in wealthy societies like those of the United States or northwestern Europe. On moral grounds, then, we could argue for a flat income tax of 90 percent to return that wealth to its real owners. In the United States, even a flat tax of 70 percent would support all governmental programs (about half the total tax) and allow payment, with the remainder, of a patrimony of about $8,000 per annum per inhabitant, or $25,000 for a family of three. This would generously leave with the original recipients of the income about three times what, according to my rough guess, they had earned.

INCENTIVES

Economists are always quick to point out that people must be properly motivated to be productive. If average returns to effort were uniformly reduced by a factor of three, it is not clear why motivation to earn more would be reduced. The behavior of two-income families in the United States suggests that the desire for income is related much more to processes of social comparison than to the real wage rate after taxes or the relative desire for goods and leisure. Similar questions may be raised about savings and capital accumulation, but in discussing them, private savings should not be dissociated from social saving (either by government or by the processes of social exchange themselves), which commonly produces externalities that are not evaluated by the market and appear nowhere in the social accounts. In any event, the questions about incentives to work and save are empirical questions that should be settled by experimentation and observation and not by philosophical debate.

I have focused on a UBI within a single nation. Let me leave aside questions of justice in reallocation of income among nations, and simply observe, as has been observed by many developmental economists, that reallocation can be accomplished at a relatively low cost by the export of knowledge rather than tangible resources. It is true that per capita income in wealthy nations might decline with increasing competition from those thereby endowed, but again, these effects of export of know-how need to be evaluated empirically and not simply posited by fiat. Meanwhile, the spread of multinational corporations, with their power to allocate capital throughout the globe, may settle the question, for better or worse, before our empirical inquiries are complete. The historical record suggests that attempts to keep technological advantages within national boundaries are not usually successful for long.

No discussion of income redistribution should conclude without considering its impact on resource conservation and population. Sustainability must be a central concern in all questions of national and global social policy. Increase in income has, in recent centuries, been the most potent means that has been found for stabilizing populations, but at the cost, alas, of increased energy production, which aggravates the problems of maintaining the quality of life on our Earth. (Bringing the Third World up to Western energy levels would multiply the carbon dioxide problem by a factor of at least ten!) We must focus on converting income and savings to forms that are more benign in this respect.

FALLING IN LOVE AGAIN

WADE RATHKE

I love this guy! I love the concept of "work fetishism." I love the notion that somebody, somewhere, somehow may really be worried about, and working on, a public program that would assure "a natural and attractive way of ensuring a fair distribution of real freedom." That may be my definition of heaven on earth. But I'm also just the kind of guy who could fall hard for the "universal basic income" scheme.

At one level it's near where I came into this fight. In the late 1960s, I was an organizer for the National Welfare Rights Organization (NWRO) in Springfield, Massachusetts, Boston, and Little Rock, Arkansas, during the founding of the Association of Community Organizations for Reform Now (ACORN). We fought tooth and nail in those days for the principal plank in the NWRO platform—a guaranteed annual income.

According to George Wiley's definition of the term and the suggestions of leaders like Johnnie Tillmon, we set the number around $5,500 per year for a family of four. We fought this campaign both in the streets and in the suites. The demonstrations were highly publicized. And the NWRO national staff pushed the debate forward by determining a real number ($5,500 or fight!) to offset the lowballing figures from economist James Tobin and the McGovern "demogrant," as well as Daniel Patrick Moynihan's $1,800 per year Guaranteed Annual Income (GAI) welfare proposal under Nixon. NWRO led the opposition to most of these proposals because they were too punitive and too small. We didn't know then that we were as close as we might ever get to a payday over this thirty-year stretch.

Today, we seem to have largely lost the battle on forced work. Workfare, as it has become under the Clinton welfare plan, is the bedrock of the program, while the notion of a guaranteed annual income for welfare recipients, much less a UBI, has been lost in the policy debate completely. Workfare is "work fetishism" with a vengeance, since the penalty for resistance—or simply noncompliance—is a guarantee of no income whatsoever.

Having been so badly routed on the issue of "distributing real freedom," organizers for low and moderate income families and communities have tried to change gears and focus more on *making work pay*. That has meant that ACORN has organized "workfare unions," particularly in Los Angeles, New York, and Milwaukee. We have fought —and sometimes won—on issues requiring the payment of minimum wages for workfare, creating rights and entitlements on workfare jobs, and winning formal grievance procedures for workfare workers. Nonetheless, people do still have to work.

Outside of the workfare regime, we believe the living-wage movement has been crucial in reintroducing the issue of wages and wage levels out of the context of a firm and its workforce and into the general policy debate. These living-wage fights have led to the passage of more than fifty city and county ordinances requiring significant wage thresholds, mostly for publicly contracted work within these communities. ACORN, Locals 100 and 880 of the Service Employees International Union, and other unions and community groups have made a huge contribution in this fight. Current efforts, like the pending initiative in New Orleans to raise the minimum wage by one dollar over the federal level for all workers in the city, could take the fight to the next level.

This work problem is real. Damned if people don't seem to *want* to work. They want to be paid fairly, treated with dignity and respect, and they want to think that their jobs are important—the whole package. It strains my imagination to think of the burgeoning service economy, chock-a-block with minimum wage and menial jobs, surviving if citizens could get paid to not work at any level, no matter how pitiful. Firms would be unable to fill some of these jobs without a gun.

So, as smitten as I am with all of this, and as hard as I have always fallen for the notion of something like the UBI, I just can't see it happening. With a projected trillion-dollar federal treasury surplus, the silence around a guaranteed annual income for everybody in the national policy debate is deafening. I think we should encourage Van Parijs and the whole UBI debate: rather than fiddle-faddling around about what might be possible, why not push the limits of the dialogue as far as we can get people to go? But the notion that we could move a consensus around income—much less freedom—as an entitlement of the American economy and work culture strikes me as an elegant and delightful fantasy.

I feel like a jaded, forlorn victim of unrequited love. I think we need more and more of this, if for nothing else, just to take the edge off.

SECURITY AND LAISSEZ-FAIRE

EMMA ROTHSCHILD

The idea of a universal subsistence income is consonant, in several respects, with the traditions of free-market political economy. One of the most powerful early pamphlets in favor of the unlimited freedom of commerce in subsistence foods—Condorcet's *Réflexions sur le commerce des blés* of 1776 —begins with an unconditional assertion: "That all members of society should have an assured subsistence each season, each year, and wherever they live . . . is the general interest of every nation."[1] It is "highly desirable, that the certainty of subsistence should be held out by law to the destitute able-bodied," John Stuart Mill wrote in 1848, in his account of the foundations and limits of laissez-faire.[2] In *The Road to Serfdom* in 1944, F. A. Hayek suggested that "the security of a minimum income," or the "certainty of a given minimum of subsistence for all," should be "provided for all outside of and supplementary to the market system."[3]

The concern with universal security of subsistence corresponded to several continuing preoccupations. One was with the relationship between markets and social institutions. Freedom in economic life—the freedom to transact, exchange, work, carry one's goods to market—was thought by Condorcet and Mill to be an end in itself, as well as a means to the end of economic opulence. It was also thought to be founded on certain political and legal circumstances. The most important had to do with the law; the "equal and impartial administration of justice which renders the rights of the meanest British subject respectable to the greatest," as Adam Smith wrote in *The Wealth of Nations*.[4] Another circumstance had to do with ways of thinking—that all members of society should be fairly enlightened, in the sense of having had at least some education, of not being intimidated by political oppression, and of being disposed, at least occasionally, to question established privileges and prejudices. These circumstances were extremely unlikely to obtain, it was believed, in a society of such inequality that some individuals were insecure even with respect to their basic subsistence.

A second preoccupation was with the causes of individual enterprise. Individual security—in the sense that no one lived so close to the margin of subsistence as to fear a sudden descent into destitution—was thought to be the best foundation for industriousness. To take risks, to move jobs, to think of new ways of making money—these were the dispositions of an enterprising society, and they were unlikely to flourish if individuals were exposed to very large and very sudden losses, such that even their subsistence was at risk. The incentives to enterprise have often been identified in terms of what Malthus described as the "hope to rise" and the "fear to fall," the reward of industry and the punishment of indolence. It is interesting that Adam Smith was concerned virtually exclusively with hopes and rewards, or with positive incentives. The thought of precariousness and insecurity was a source of "anxious and desponding moments." Fear was "a wretched instrument of government." When individuals were profoundly discouraged, for Mill, "assistance is a tonic, not a sedative."

A third preoccupation was with the simplicity of policy. Smith and Condorcet were harshly critical of the regulations of the commercial system. These regulations were inefficient, and they were also unjust. They provided almost limitless scope for "vexatious" investigations of individual citizens, for "visitations" of their homes, for "the inspections, the prohibitions, the condemnations, the vexations" that were for Condorcet characteristic of city life. The provisions of the English Poor Laws, in Smith's description, were such as to obstruct the freedom of movement of the poor. The poor were subject to "the caprice of any churchwarden or overseer," and to being arbitrarily moved in an "evident violation of natural liberty and justice." Government should be reduced, in Condorcet's opinion, to the "smallest possible quantity." But it should also be made much more simple. There should be relief for misery when it could not be prevented. There should be an end to the "humiliation attached to poverty."

All of these eighteenth- and nineteenth-century arguments provide good reasons to take very seriously Van Parijs's proposal for a universal basic income. The UBI would be likely to improve the social conditions for economic competition. It would be likely to make at least some individuals more enterprising, in that it would reduce the fear of extreme deprivation, or of uncertainty with respect to subsistence income. It would be easy to understand, and inexpensive in administrative costs. It would be equitable, in that it would provide relatively little opportunity for the vexatious and oppressive use of complicated regulations. It would hold out the promise of universal security, in the sense that every individual could be sure that her situation, while it might become worse, would never fall below a level of minimum subsistence.

The eighteenth-century economists' own policies for increasing security were substantially different from the UBI. Condorcet, in the 1790s, proposed a combination of social insurance, education, emergency relief, and a universal system of savings banks, whereby even the smallest, daily savings could be deposited securely (a sort of micro-credit, with the poor as the creditors). Social policies of this sort are complementary to a UBI, and would continue to be important even if a UBI were implemented. The objective of increasing universal security of subsistence does not require a UBI. A UBI might indeed increase inequality, if it were financed by a reduction in social expenditures, or in transfer payments to the elderly and the infirm, or in emergency relief.

Any society, or at least any society in which a subsistence

income is substantially less than the average income, can in principle afford a UBI. In the United States, government transfer payments now cost about $1 trillion per year, or the equivalent of more than $5,000 for every adult resident. But the effects of a UBI would be highly sensitive to the level of income provided. A UBI of $5,000 per year, for example, would be likely to have very little effect on the insidious "unemployment trap" that Van Parijs describes. The definition of a subsistence income is elusive (as the extended eighteenth-century disputes over necessities and luxuries suggested), and a UBI that had a substantial effect on the subjective sense of security of the very young might have almost no effect on the lives of older people. Its principal effect might be to reduce inequality, including the inequality of insecurity, across different groups of young people: those who go to university and those who do not; those who are within the prison and penal system and those who are not; those who are employed and those who are unemployed; those who vote and those who do not.

The most important promise of a UBI—and an important cost, as well—seems to me to be political. The existence of extreme poverty and insecurity, like the existence of extreme opulence, was thought by some of the early theorists of laissez-faire to pose very serious problems for political life. The very rich could buy political power through regulations that favored their own enterprises, privileges (or private laws), changes in public opinion, changes in the rules of market games. This was an obstruction, it was thought, to the efficient operation of economic competition, and to democratic political institutions. The very poor, in the *ancien régime,* were excluded from political power on the grounds (among others) that they were dependent on other people, they had no time to become educated, and they had no interest in the great questions of public life or in the future of the society. The equality of rights, Condorcet wrote during the French Revolution, would be no more than a "ghostly imposture" if large numbers of people continued to subsist on insufficient and uncertain resources and were subject to "that inequality which brings a real dependence."

The democratic institutions of the most developed countries of the twenty-first century are not an imposture. But they are weakened, in important ways, by the power of money in electoral politics, and by the powerlessness, the voluntary or imposed exclusion, of the poor and the young. The percentage of persons voting in the 1996 U.S. presidential election varied from 75 percent for white males aged sixty-five to seventy-four, to 12 percent for Hispanic-origin males aged eighteen to twenty-four. This is not a flourishing political society. It is a society of inequality in the exercise of political rights. The inequality of income, and of security with respect to subsistence income, is only one among many explanations for this incapacity. But the security of (present and future) subsistence to which a UBI could contribute—a security that would include even the

{ 48 }

indolent and the undeserving and the imprisoned—holds some promise, at least, of political renewal.

The costs of the UBI are also political, in a different and wider sense. Van Parijs starts by saying that "everyone should be paid a universal subsistence income." I take this "everyone" to be truly universal, to include everyone, everywhere in the international or global society. But this is a distant objective. I think it is fairly reasonable to expect that a society of greater and more universal justice would also be a society that was more open to individuals and influences from other societies. Individuals who have a strong sense of living in a society of equals are perhaps more likely to have a sense that they live in the same (international) society as other, distant people. But in the short term, at least, the effort to ensure universal security in one or more rich societies might pose quite serious difficulties for freedom of movement between countries, and for the freedom (including freedom from "vexatious" prohibitions) of registered and unregistered residents.[5] A UBI might make the inequality between individuals in different societies more obvious, and more oppressive.

One political challenge, now, is to make democratic institutions more engaging and more inclusive. The other challenge is to make them more international—to invent political institutions in which individuals in different countries participate on the basis of equal rights. My concern about the UBI scheme is that it would be helpful in terms of one challenge, and unhelpful in terms of the other. It is difficult to imagine a global political procedure, open and equal, in which it was determined that there should be very different levels of UBI for individuals in different societies. I hope that ideas of universal security of subsistence can "inspire and guide more modest immediate reforms," as Van Parijs writes. I also hope that they can contribute, eventually, to a politics of global inclusion.

SUBSIDIZE WAGES

EDMUND S. PHELPS

Several economists over the past couple of decades have been calling for a universal employment subsidy—a subsidy to firms for each low-wage person they employ without regard to parental or marital status. Self-support (vs. dependency), personal growth (vs. disengagement), integration (vs. marginalization)—these are our rallying cries. Now there come efforts to gain instead a reconsideration of a universal basic income, or demogrant—a periodic transfer payment to each resident with no conditions on working and earning. These two proposed innovations in social policy differ importantly, I will argue, in what they suppose a society is for. And they also rest on quite different assessments of the practical consequences they would have, if adopted.

In several ways I find the idea of a demogrant attractive, as I did when, in the 1960s, I was a young economist just beginning to think about economic and social policy. A demogrant would help to level the playing field by counteracting the ability of families—under market socialism and market capitalism—to bequeath their children advantages (such as individual freedom) over other children, their children's children, etc. A demogrant would permit low-wage workers to reject as inadequate the pay differentials offered by unsafe

{ 51 }

or unhealthy jobs. It would also bring an efficiency gain in giving people more of their total social benefit in the form of fungible cash to use as they prefer, and less in the form of free services whose amounts are chosen by the state. One can therefore understand the support that proposals for a demogrant usually find.

The idea of a universal minimum income seems to enjoy especially wide appeal among the many Europeans who have an almost religious (and, in many cases, literally religious) sense of nation and community. To them it will appear to be further progress in the development of a society that feels the near-sacred value of each person's life and autonomy. Most of Western Europe, particularly the Continent, has already gone a long way toward providing universal—that is, unconditional—benefits to its citizens (and in most cases other residents): subsidized housing, free medical care and free education services, among other services.

Now Philippe Van Parijs makes the strongest imaginable case for going the rest of the way by means of a universal basic income. But I remain opposed. For me, there are two sticking points. One of them, which I will take up later, has to do with consequences. The demogrant device has no monopoly on the beneficial effects that make us like it, whatever the balance of its total benefits and total cost. The alternative to it—a subsidy to employers for every low-wage worker in their full-time employ—would have some of those effects and some other benefits as well. The subsidy, in pulling up paychecks and the number employed at the low-

{ 52 }

wage end of the labor market, would mitigate serious disadvantages of talent and background; it would expand the jobs that low earners could afford to reject; and it would widen low earners' latitude in meeting their needs.

The other sticking point is that the demogrant idea seems in an important respect to go against the grain of the traditional American conception of a liberal republic. This conception, I will argue, would cause many Americans to hesitate to embrace a universal basic income while being willing, at least in principle, to contemplate low-wage employment subsidies.

Let's consider these two points, starting with the second.

1. Where can we look for the American conception of the liberal society? I suggest we need look no farther than John Rawls, widely regarded to be the leading moral philosopher of the twentieth century. His *A Theory of Justice* is seen by many as the sourcebook of most of the new ideas of importance on how to think about matters of justice in economic and social policy, even if we don't always want to follow him to the letter. Since Rawls is an American writing against the background of American social history, the conception of society he expresses in that book is at least an important sample of American thinking.

The conception of liberal society there is in refreshing contrast to the more European one. It excludes religious states having a public purpose. It also excludes aggregations of persons engaged in solitary pursuits who might cooperate only for their mutual protection. For Rawls, a society (the sort of society he wants to consider, at any rate) is a cooperative enterprise in which individuals come together to participate in its interactive economy for the purpose of mutual private gain—largely, individual achievement and personal growth from career and family life. Accordingly, economic justice is about the distribution of those mutual gains among the individuals participating. It is wrongheaded to ask what this economic justice requires in the way of support for individuals who choose to opt out and live in isolation off the land, or sects that choose to break off from the larger society. Rawls's kind of justice is owed only to those who, being able and willing, participate and contribute at least something to the economy's pie.[1]

These views on the nature and function of society trace far back in American thought. Thomas Jefferson wrote that the early settlers came to the American continent for "the acquisition & free possession of property"—and for the "pursuit of happiness" in the process, as he was to say later. Calvin Coolidge encapsulated the cooperative-enterprise conception of society with his great apothegm, "the business of America is business." It came to be understood in the Progressive Era that the possibility of mutual gain, which Rawls built on, arose from the "social surplus" generated by the interaction of people's diverse talents and skills within society's central institution, the business economy. In his economics textbook, which was dominant for nearly the second half of the last century, Paul Samuelson never failed to bring up this social surplus, always citing the eloquent statement of the idea by the social theorist L. T. Hobhouse in his 1922 book *The Elements of Social Justice.* It is implicit, I think, that the social surplus is a flow of income that can be legitimately redistributed, since the way a free market would distribute it is morally arbitrary and a free market is an impossibility in any case.[2] It is also implicit in all these expressions, I believe, that the social surplus is to be made available for redistribution to the contributors, not to noncontributors. It would be incoherent to say that the contributors to society's enterprise, in generating a social surplus, have—as defenders of a UBI suggest—the obligation to share it with those who have not contributed. What do the latter have to do with it? If they can be shown somehow to have a claim, is there a claim of animals and other sentient creatures? If we earth people should discover Martians unwilling to trade or collaborate with us, do they nonetheless have a claim too?

2. The argument for UBI set out by Van Parijs appears to be substantially pragmatic. He appears to believe that, although it might go against the ideology of some to hand out the basic income *unconditionally,* the practical *effect* of doing so will be to encourage participation, hard work, self-support, achievement, and all the other desiderata dear to those with that perspective.

A UBI, Van Parijs writes, "makes it easier to take a break between two jobs, reduce working time, make room for more training, take up self-employment, or join a cooperative. And with a UBI, workers will only take a job if they find it suitably attractive, while employer subsidies make unattractive, low-productivity jobs more economically viable."

One can see that a UBI would open up some new job options to many people, just as inheriting a substantial sum of money would make it possible to try one's hand at composing music or writing a book. But financing it will entail lower after-tax wages and lower private saving until private wealth (defined to exclude the present discounted value of the expected stream of UBI) has reached a sufficiently reduced level; to a rough approximation, private wealth would fall by as much as social wealth (defined as the present value of the UBI stream) rose.

So there is no alchemy here by which a net increase of wealth is achieved and costlessly at that. At some point in middle age, the *average* worker-saver will have a lower *total* wealth, private plus social, than he or she would otherwise have had, since wealth per head (which I am taking to be unchanged) is an average of the wealth per head of the young, who now get their social wealth right off the bat, and the wealth per head of the old. The contention that there is a social gain from "moving up" people's wealth to the first year of adulthood, since the increased liquidity serves to increase freedom, depends on the assumption that the social benefit from the added liquidity is sufficiently large to overcome the social cost resulting from the reduction of after-tax rewards to working.

Of course the main part of the argument is redistributive: the increased wealth would occur among those with little, the reduction of wealth would occur among those with much. But a low-wage employment subsidy scheme also would be redistributive in the same direction. So we must weigh the practical balance of benefits and costs posed by the UBI against the corresponding balance offered by low-wage employment subsidies. I see some serious drawbacks of a UBI; these drawbacks mirror the merits of low-wage employment subsidies.

I'll emphasize four drawbacks. First, the pay rates available to low-wage workers are already so low as to be demoralizing. A large UBI would seem towering to a low-wage worker, and would further depreciate his or her earning power; moreover, the UBI, in requiring higher taxation to finance it, would tend to reduce their net pay rates further. Worsened employee performance would follow and, since firms won't create jobs for workers who will quit or shirk or are absent at the drop of a hat, a large number of jobs held by low-wage workers in private business would become extinct.

Second, we are in dire straits to begin with in this regard. Work, career, and achievement are already threatened by a whole array of competitors—crime, unemployment, and the underground economy.[3] This is no time to launch a new scheme that would create further disincentives to work in the legitimate business economy. Marginalization must be *reduced,* not increased. Introducing a UBI would make that task harder.

Third, what matters to people is not just their total receipts; it is the self-support from *earning their own way.* No amount of UBI would substitute for the satisfaction of having earned one's way without help from parents, friends and the state—as valued as they are. I would note that, if the UBI were adopted in the United States, it would continue to rankle low-wage earners that their pay was less than half the median wage. The reason it would, I suggest, is that low-wage workers would view such low relative pay rates as bluntly showing that they cannot hope to earn their own way in the sense of gaining access to most of the median earners' way of life *through their own earning;* they can only gain access through the demogrant, which they may see as demeaning.

Finally, what about Parijs's image of the workplace with its exhausted women and tyrannical bosses? I feel that many academics and others reared in relatively privileged circumstances cannot see how those working in a factory for forty hours a week could value it as a means to mix and interact with others, to gain a sense of belonging in the community, and to have a sense of contributing something to the country's collective project, which is business. If I am right on these matters, we should feel sorry, not envious, about Van Parijs's surfer who feels lucky to be able to drop out of the world of work thanks to his UBI; he doesn't know what he is missing. And we shouldn't feel sorry about women "subjected to the dictates of a boss for forty hours a week." They have the self-knowledge to know something that Van Parijs appears not to know about them: the sociability, the challenges, and the sense of contribution and belonging that those jobs provide are an important part of their lives, as they are of the lives of others.

The problem is that the low-end pay rates are much too low, so low that some low-end workers must take the least "liberating" jobs to make ends meet. The solution is not to endow workers with a UBI, so that they move to somewhat better jobs at a reduction in pay or else just drop out. That way lies dependency, unfulfillment, depression, and marginalization. The solution is to institute a low-wage employment subsidy, so that all pay rates facing low-wage workers would be pulled up to levels better reflecting the social productivity of their employment, their support of themselves, and their development. Then low-wage men and women could afford to avoid dangerous, unhealthy, or oppressive jobs and opt instead for more rewarding work. And many more people would be able to know the satisfactions of self-support, development, participation, and contribution.

UBI AND THE WORK ETHIC

BRIAN BARRY

General Motors is expecting sales approaching 150,000 per year for the Hummer, a four-seater vehicle of military origin that is more than seven feet wide, weighs more than seven thousand pounds, and scores extremely poorly on fuel efficiency and pollution criteria. Designed to negotiate vertical walls twenty-two inches high, its road clearance makes it likely to override the bumpers of a car in a collision, thus enabling its weight (about three times that of a car) to do maximum damage to the car's occupants. And where does General Motors hope to sell these juggernauts? "You'll see a lot in New York City, places like Manhattan where your affluent buyers are," the *New York Times* quotes the general manager of Hummer operations as saying. "Paul Bellow, GM's general director of market analysis, said that the rising concentration of wealth and income in America over the last two decades had been the most important social trend for automakers. A very large class of high-income, fairly youthful households had been created, he said, and these people care little about gasoline and other vehicle operating expenses"—or, presumably, the $93,000 price tag that General Motors is proposing to attach to the Hummer.[1]

What would be needed to make this kind of antisocial

toy a commercial nonstarter? Any solution must proceed in two directions. One is the taxation of income, wealth, and inheritance to offset the huge gains made at the top end of the distribution of income in the past twenty years, and the other is to bring the tax on gasoline at least up to Western European levels. These two measures are desirable in themselves. Moreover, backed up by other "green" taxes to cut energy use, they would generate so much revenue as to go much of the way toward answering the usual first question about any basic income proposal: "Where's the money to come from?" The notion that the money raised should go to everybody equally could appeal to both right and left, the one because the money is not spent on government programs and the other because it helps most those with the least. This is not to deny, of course, that there are other places in the world in which a subsistence-level basic income for everybody (even by local standards of subsistence) could probably be achieved only by transfers from outside. I believe that a compelling moral case can be made out for the proposition that poor countries whose public administration is honest and competent enough to deliver a basic income should be helped to do so by rich countries in a systematic way. I shall, however, follow Van Parijs in focusing on the United States, with some side-glances at Western Europe.

It need hardly be said that it is one thing to identify where the money could come from and another to explain where the political motivation to raise it is to be found. A time of serious proposals to cut income taxes, abolish the inheritance tax, and even reduce the gas tax is less than propitious. We should bear in mind, however, that sometimes things move a lot faster and a lot further—and a lot sooner—than is generally expected. In politics, as in geology, seismic events resist prophecy. In a spirit of speculation, however, let me mention three conceivable ways in which a move to a universal basic income could be precipitated.

Imagine, then, some kind of really dramatic evidence of global warming—the disappearance of a medium-sized Pacific island under the sea, for example. This just might jolt public opinion into support for massive energy taxes. Returning the revenue to everybody equally would just by itself constitute a basic income at some level or other.

A second candidate is a revulsion against the U.S. "war on drugs," which currently incarcerates more people than are in jail from all causes in the European Union, which has a hundred million more inhabitants. Of course, the thought of the prisons being emptied and a lot of young or youngish unemployed (and maybe hard to employ) males returning home might well send shivers up some spines, but at the same time shutting down most of the prisons would make a great deal of money available. If we want to identify a forerunner to basic income in American politics, Richard Nixon's Family Assistance Plan is, I suggest, more relevant than anything mentioned by Van Parijs in that it almost became law. Its architect, Daniel Patrick Moynihan, made no bones about the cynicism of its motivation: paying people not to work is cheaper than job-creation schemes, and buying off violence is cheaper than suppressing it. Both of these maxims retain their validity and could lead to a revival of interest in unconditional income support if concern for the stability of the inner cities resurfaced.

Finally, the inequality of income and wealth may become so great, with so much money in the hands of such a small proportion of the population, that the logic of electoral competition will impel the Democrats to play the redistribution card. That leaves open the question of the form redistribution might take, which is precisely why the pros and cons of basic income need to be argued during an unpromising period such as the present.

Asking about the pros and cons of basic income as such is rather like asking about the pros and cons of keeping a feline as a pet without distinguishing between a tiger and a tabby. Basic income has very different characteristics at different levels. Many of the advantages that Van Parijs claims for a basic income scheme would be realized only if it were pitched at subsistence level (or higher). Thus, for example, the uncertainty that inhibits people from moving from unemployment benefit (and, even more, disability benefit) would be allayed only if the unconditional alternative were enough to live on. Similarly, only a basic income at (or approaching) subsistence level would enable people to take time between jobs, get more training, or start a new business. Again, workers can refuse "desperation" jobs and women can leave abusive husbands only if the alternative income is adequate. The same goes for the possibility of engaging in full-time caring for children or for elderly or infirm relatives.

Despite this, the level of basic income actually plays no part in Van Parijs's arguments for it. He says at one point that he "favor[s] the highest sustainable such income," and adds that in the richer countries this level exceeds a reasonable definition of subsistence. But there is really no way of guessing what the highest level of basic income would be in any country after all the changes in employment and taxation had settled down into an equilibrium. If Van Parijs is right, though, we have to ask about the pros and cons of a basic income at a level higher than "a reasonable definition of subsistence." These are different from those of either a basic income below or one at subsistence level. In the end, I will defend a subsistence level basic income, in preference to Van Parijs's proposal.

Let me begin with the least demanding reform: introduction of a basic income at below subsistence level. If we are concerned about the "Malibu surfer" problem—the prospect of able-bodied people with employable skills choosing to live a life of self-indulgence, albeit at subsistence level—then maintaining the basic income below subsistence level solves it. Unfortunately, however, it yields only in an attenuated form at best the advantages offered by a subsistence-level income that I quoted from Van Parijs. Moreover, the entire apparatus of welfare benefits would still have to remain in place, though benefits would, of course, be reduced by the amount of the basic income. Even here, however, the news is not all bad: in Britain, for example, the eminent economist Tony Atkinson has calculated that a basic income at a rate of half the standard state benefit would take millions of people off means-tested benefits, which are demoralizing, demeaning, and expensive to administer.

I have already listed a number of the advantages of a subsistence-level basic income. Moreover, its relation to the work ethic is not as one-sided as might appear at first blush. It is true that it reinstates the "Malibu surfer" problem. But at the same time it definitively abolishes the "poverty trap" that leads all traditional welfare systems down the path of coercion. The point of a basic income is that, in contrast to a conditional welfare benefit, it is not lost by taking a job. The result is that even very poorly paid work makes you better off than not working. Moreover, contingent benefits criminalize a large proportion of the population for working while drawing benefit, even though they could not live on what this work brings in. The middle class in Britain is engaged in mass collusion with the officially unemployed to get houses cleaned, gardens dug, and children minded. And neither party to the transaction normally feels the slightest guilt—nor should they. There is surely something crazy about the stipulation that those drawing unemployment benefit must be "available for work" at any moment, which rules out their using the time to improve their qualifications, engage in community work, or help a neighbor while earning a bit extra. This is, in my view, the knock-down argument for basic income at subsistence level.

From this point of view, the Malibu surfers are a drawback, but one worth putting up with for the advantages that are inseparable from the unconditionality of a basic income. A superficially attractive way of getting at the surfers while maintaining many of the advantages of a subsistence-level basic income is Atkinson's proposal of a "participation income." As one reviewer explains, "Atkinson defines participation to include: paid employment; self-employment; full-time education or training; intensive care work and approved forms of voluntary work."[2] But this opens up a nightmarish scenario of an enormous bureaucracy entrusted with arbitrary monitoring powers. My guess is that something like "participation income" might be necessary politically to get a basic income introduced, but that the expense and intrusiveness of administering it (as well as its lending itself so easily to fraud) would lead either to abandoning the whole experiment or moving to an unconditional basic income.

All this presupposes, of course, that surfers really are a drawback. For Van Parijs, they are from a practical point of view, since the more of them there are the lower the sustainable unconditional income will be. Clearly, his surmise that in wealthy countries the maximum sustainable basic income would be well above any reasonable definition of subsistence level presupposes that the proportion of the population who could contribute significantly to the economy and choose not to, would not be very large.

But what Van Parijs does not make altogether clear in his essay is that he rejects the idea that those who take a basic income (even one well above subsistence level) and do nothing for the community should be subject to reproach. As Van Parijs says at the start of his essay, he wishes to maintain that the highest possible unconditional basic income is an entitlement derived from a theory of justice conceived in terms of "real freedom for all." In the essay, he only hints at the nature of this theory, laid out in his book *Real Freedom for All*, and I cannot undertake to expound it in any detail here. I *can* say that by "real freedom" Van Parijs means (roughly) the ability to do what you want, and that his criterion of justice is that the freedom of those with the least real freedom is to be maximized. The means to real freedom so defined are resources, so (again, roughly) this means that the resources available to those with the least should be maximized. Those with the least are those who do nothing to generate any income for themselves by their own efforts. Hence, the size of the unconditional basic income is what should be maximized.

Why is this just? Van Parijs has several answers to this question. One is that it is unfair if those who are congenitally lazy have a smaller chance to get what they want than those who are more inclined to work. But we do not believe that people with antisocial traits (strong dispositions towards, say, rape or pedophilia) should have as much chance to fulfill their desires as others, and if the wish to live at others' expense is an antisocial trait there is no reason for making special efforts to indulge it.

Another argument is that everybody living in a country is entitled to an equal share of "external assets," which underwrites a 100 percent rate of estate duty. Van Parijs then extends the notion of an "external asset" by calling on the theory of "efficiency wages," according to which it is profitable for employers to offer wages at above a market-clearing rate to induce employees to want to keep their jobs. As a result, there are always some people who could equally well do any given job and would be prepared to do it for less than those who hold the jobs are getting. On the basis of this, Van Parijs deduces that income tax rates should be set to produce the maximum possible yield: people who hold the well-paying jobs are beneficiaries of good fortune, and cannot object to having that good fortune taxed. Putting these two taxes together produces the revenue whose amplitude arouses such optimism in him.

The argument is unconvincing. It is hard to see why those who have no intention of engaging in paid employment should have any claim on the proceeds of a tax whose rationale is to offset the good fortune of those who have well-paid jobs at the expense of others who are just as qualified and would like to be doing them instead.

If I am right, then, the arguments that Van Parijs offers for the justice of maximizing the size of the basic income are defective. In their absence, I do not believe that there is any good case for pushing the demand for a basic income above the subsistence level. Of course, the notion of "subsistence" is still negotiable. It must be redefined for each society, so as to include the diet, amenities, and access to services that are widely thought to be necessary to "get along." It should also provide the material conditions for participating in the social and political life of the community. Something approaching a consensus has emerged in Western Europe that an income of half the median is, as a rule of thumb, what is needed to meet these criteria. Endorsing, then, the proposal for an unconditional basic income at subsistence level, let me conclude by offering that interpretation of it.

OPTIONAL FREEDOMS

ELIZABETH ANDERSON

Philippe Van Parijs advocates the provision of the maximum sustainable unconditional basic income. His defense rests on a political philosophy that he calls "real libertarianism." I shall argue that Van Parijs's real libertarianism cannot justify a UBI, but that a UBI may have some promise as a supplementary part of a larger social welfare package that is justified on other grounds.

A policy to enact and maximize a UBI, conceived as a means to real libertarianism, suffers from three defects. First, it favors distributing income over direct in-kind provision of, or vouchers for, particular goods, such as health care or education. The preference for income rather than in-kind transfers reflects the commitment of real libertarianism to promoting freedom, conceived as a generic good; the real libertarian urges that we provide people with the resources they need to achieve their aims, whatever those aims are. Thus it gives no special priority to freedom from disease over the freedom to idle: freedom is freedom. As an account of what we owe to one another, that seems misguided. What we owe are not the means to generic freedom but the social conditions of the particular, concrete freedoms that are instrumental to life in relations of equality with others. We owe each other the rights, institutions, social norms, public goods, and private resources that people need to avoid oppression (social exclusion, violence, exploitation, and so forth) and to exercise the capabilities necessary for functioning as equal citizens in a democratic state.[1] From a social point of view, then, we should grant higher priority to securing certain goods, such as education, over others, such as surfing opportunities, even if some individuals prefer surfing to schooling. A maximal UBI risks overproviding optional freedoms at a substantial sacrifice—large enough to compromise social equality—to the particular freedoms we owe one another.

Second, in providing equal levels of income to all, the UBI does not adjust for the fact that, due to variations in internal traits, social roles, and other circumstances, some people are better able to convert income to freedoms than others.[2] Disabled people typically require more resources to achieve equivalent freedoms—to move around, to get access to information, and so forth—than those who are not disabled. People who engage in unpaid dependent care work also require more resources to achieve equivalent freedoms to those who do not take care of dependents. (For example, to be free to participate in the realm of paid labor, they need access to alternative sources of care for their dependents while they work.) The UBI therefore best serves the interests of healthy adults who care for no one besides themselves. In taking income, rather than capabilities, to be the relevant space in which equality is to be pursued, the UBI assumes as the norm for human beings the perspective of the healthy, egoistic adult.

Third, in granting a basic income that is not conditioned on the willingness of the able to work, the UBI promotes freedom without responsibility, and thereby both offends and undermines the ideal of social obligation that undergirds the welfare state. A UBI would not only inspire a segment of the able population—largely young, healthy, unattached adults—to abjure work for a life of idle fun. It would also depress the willingness to produce and pay taxes of those who resent having to support them.

To deal with the first two problems, Van Parijs could argue that the UBI should be maximized only after the social provision of particularly important freedoms, such as public education and medical care, was secured, and that supplementary programs could give extra help to people with "special" needs. In the U.S. context, at least, this contrast between universal and "special" programs has typically led to underfinanced, stigmatizing support for those regarded as "special" (for example, contrast Medicare with Medicaid). But this contrast is simply an artifact of an accounting system that measures equality in terms of income rather than particular capabilities. From the standpoint of the particular capabilities people need to avoid oppression and stand as equals in society—things such as literacy, mobility, and health—everyone has the same needs.

The social insurance programs that form the foundation

of modern welfare states constitute the terms of a great social contract. Like any insurance, they purchase a right to provision from others conditional on a willingness to provide for others, if one is able. Like any insurance, its recipients have an obligation to mitigate damages in recognition of the burdens they place on others. The social-democratic contract recognizes that over the course of a whole life, we are all dependent on caretaking by others for long periods in childhood, sickness, and old age, and some are dependent for their whole lives. This inter-generational contract is sustained and legitimated only by a recognition on the part of the able of an obligation to work and provide for the dependent and those who care for them. It is hard to see how such a contract can be sustained by a system that advertises as one of its virtues that it would free the able to live in idleness.

Suppose, however, we detached the UBI from its real-libertarian rationale. Could a UBI play a supplemental role in a welfare state founded on social insurance principles? Here we face a set of tradeoffs, with respect both to administrability and legitimacy. A UBI would not target expenditures to those who need them most, and would therefore both underprovide benefits and waste public expenditures on those who don't need them. Given high resistance to additional tax burdens, especially in North America, the risk is that such waste comes at the cost of other programs that could do more for the disadvantaged, the disabled, dependents, and those who care for them.

On the other hand, a UBI saves on the substantial administrative costs of targeting expenditures to these groups, and avoids the temptation to add demeaning and intrusive conditions to the receipt of public funds to ensure that the needy are "deserving." A UBI would have the advantage of being universal, and therefore undercut resentment of needy recipients, but the disadvantage of being unconditional, thereby inspiring resentment of undeserving recipients. It is telling that the only current example of a UBI is based on the distribution of Alaskan oil royalties: Americans, at least, don't resent unearned income, as long as it is attached to property ownership. This suggests that the legitimation problem in the United States could be solved by funding the UBI through revenues collected from the use of public property: the leasing of national forests and rangeland, oil and mining royalties, the periodic auction of temporary broadcasting licenses, and pollution taxes. Such a strategy would, however, ground the UBI on a principle of ownership rather than need, and also create public incentives to permit increased despoilment of public goods for the sake of private, if evenly distributed, gains. The main question is whether programs more carefully tailored to the needs of the disabled, the disadvantaged, dependents, and their caretakers—and to the particular freedoms we owe one another—would be more effective in delivering the promised goods, and win greater acceptance, than a UBI. I am not persuaded that the costs to the goals of social democracy would be worth the gains provided by a UBI, but I am open to empirical evidence to the contrary.

GOOD FOR WOMEN

ANNE L. ALSTOTT

Philippe Van Parijs's proposal deserves serious consideration in the United States. A universal basic income has
much to offer, particularly to women. A UBI could help fill
the gaps in U.S. social programs that leave women economically vulnerable. And the tax increase needed to fund the
program poses no serious threat to the economy. The libertarian right will surely howl that "high taxes" dramatically
reduce work and savings. But economic research challenges
that prediction. Raising the right taxes, to fund the right
programs, can render freedom and equality compatible with
economic growth.

Refreshingly, Van Parijs argues the case for the UBI in
terms of freedom—a value too seldom invoked in American
social welfare policy. For similar reasons, Bruce Ackerman
and I have proposed stakeholding—a one-time, unconditional grant to young citizens. Although stakeholding and
the UBI differ in important ways, I want to focus on their
shared strengths: both proposals could enhance women's
freedom and economic security by breaking the link between social-welfare benefits and paid work.[1]

* * *

American women face two distinctive economic risks. First, they still take primary responsibility for child care and adjust their working lives to accommodate family needs. Second, and not coincidentally, women earn about 75 percent of what men earn. The combination of child care and low earnings translates into lifelong economic insecurity. Although women's rising rates of workforce participation have improved their economic prospects, the average woman's career remains shorter, more disrupted, and less remunerative than the average man's.

Despite these well-known facts, neither welfare nor Social Security adequately addresses women's distinctive situation. Consider two examples. First are the single mothers. In 1998, one quarter of U.S. families with children were headed by women. Their median income was just $22,000, even though nearly 80 percent of single mothers were in the labor force. Almost forty percent of single-mother families were poor in 1998. And welfare offers only meager support. Welfare reforms in the mid-1990s adopted the faulty premise that poor single mothers just need to "get a job." In the typical state, welfare families now face a five-year lifetime time limit, and in the meantime collect benefits of just $700 per month. The booming economy and the phase-in of time limits have cushioned the transition to the new rules. But, at best, most welfare mothers will work in low-wage jobs that pay too little to support a family.

As a second example, consider the plight of older women.

In 1998, 13 percent of elderly women were poor, compared to 7 percent of elderly men. The median income of elderly men is $18,000, compared to $10,000 for elderly women. The disparity reflects not only women's longer average life span, but also the residual effects of divorce, child-care responsibilities, and low earnings. The Social Security program has two serious flaws. First, benefits presume a lifelong work history, so women who interrupt paid work to rear children lose out. Second, although the program includes an extra benefit for wives, the rules work best for women in lifelong marriages with male breadwinners. The result is a notable gender gap. In 1998, women workers received less ($675 per month, on average) than male retirees ($877)—while women who claimed benefits as wives got just $400 per month.

In contrast, a UBI offers benefits without a time limit, without a work test, and without a marriage test. Even a UBI below subsistence level could make a real difference in women's lives. In 1999, for example, the poverty line for one person was about $8,500. Consider a UBI of less than half, or $4,000. For the median single mother, that would mean an 18 percent increase in income—for the median elderly woman, a 40 percent increase.

And the UBI comes without strings, so women can choose for themselves how to spend the cash. For example, some single mothers would use the money to work harder. They might buy better food or housing, a car to get to work, or better day care. Others would trade money for time, by quitting a second job or taking a job with a shorter commute but lower pay. The UBI places that choice squarely where it belongs—with women.

The key virtue of the UBI is that it breaks the link between benefits and paid work. In contrast, fashionable reforms like the earned income tax credit (EITC) and "privatized" Social Security take the wrong direction. The EITC is more humane than welfare, supplementing low wages without a time limit. But the EITC is paid only while one works—and in proportion to wages. Those who take time off, who work part-time, or who go back to school lose some or all their benefits. Social Security is more complex, because "privatization" connotes many different reforms. But the major plans would continue or strengthen the relationship between lifetime wages and retirement benefits. Indeed, some of the proposals would provide less protection for women than Social Security now does.[2] In contrast, a UBI would ensure that everyone can count on the same income floor, regardless of work history.

As Van Parijs anticipates, critics will worry that the taxes needed to fund a UBI would reduce economic growth. In response, Van Parijs rightly questions the assumption that growth should trump freedom and equality. Maximizing growth for the benefit of richer future generations should not come at the expense of justice for today.

But advocates of the UBI can also challenge the factual basis of the anti-tax critique. Higher taxes to fund the right kind of program are compatible with economic growth. First, studies suggest that most workers and savers would not change their behavior much in response to higher income taxes.[3] Second, as Van Parijs emphasizes, the UBI could promote growth by freeing people to be more productive. To be sure, some would use their UBI to work shorter hours; I have just argued that this option might be particularly valuable for mothers. But others might use the UBI to take time off for education or training. Third, although income, wealth, and estate taxes redistribute most effectively from rich to poor, progressives should be open to alternative levies that produce an *overall* redistribution in the direction of the less well off. For example, consumption taxes and environmental taxes might appeal to a wider political coalition. These taxes look regressive if one focuses on the tax burden alone. But if combined with a UBI, they could work a net redistribution that is quite progressive.

Van Parijs offers a welcome challenge to the fixation on paid work that pervades American social welfare policy. The UBI can deliver what Van Parijs promises: real freedom for *all*—including women.

DIGNITY AND DEPRIVATION

RONALD DORE

Philippe Van Parijs proposes a basic income at a level that might be politically feasible in the short term—something that, as he says, would not provide a comfortable standard of living on its own. I think, rather, of the basic income movement as preparing the ground for a future society, two or three decades hence, in which a much higher level of basic income will become possible. Let me suggest what sort of society that might be, and then say why I find it attractive.

Such a society would have to be productive enough, and would have to have sufficient consensus in favor of redistribution to devote, say, 40 percent of GNP to giving everyone a citizen's income, as of right. No dole, no means tests, no concept of unemployment. The market economy goes on. Those who want to work and are genetically lucky enough to be able to learn skills that the market rewards, do so and have more than the basic income to spend. Those who do not work include the genetically unlucky, who would find it hard to get a job, as well as those who are capable of almost anything but prefer to write poetry or play chess. Nobody bothers much which person is which. Citizenship involves duties of community service as well as a right to the basic income. There is a wide range of voluntary choice in the form of community service, but you make an annual service return as well as an income tax return, and the safeguards against cheating are similar in both cases.

I find such a society attractive for several reasons.

1. I belong to the same generation as Mrs. Thatcher, so when she and her ministers were railing at the welfare dependent, and saying how they *ought* to feel ashamed of themselves, I knew exactly what she meant. Except that instead of "ought to" I would have said that "they probably *do*" feel ashamed of themselves—especially if they *were* trying to find a job, and were finding that potential employers counted them as unemployable, and that the Social Security office (suspecting them of concealing some undisclosed income or a fraudulently undeclared contributing boyfriend) treated them like dirt.

No rich society ought to inflict such a loss of personal dignity on people who, with no externally obvious disability, have come out of their families and schools with such low helpings of energy, self-confidence, beauty, brainpower, or chutzpah that they are always among the last in the competition for jobs.

A basic income would obscure the distinction between those who would find it difficult to get a job and those who simply prefer to live modestly in order to play at being shepherds in the morning and literary critics in the afternoon.

That should help with the dignity problem, which in my view is at least as serious an aspect of unemployment as the poverty problem.

To be sure, I know that there are whole subcultures in our society that wholly reject the norms on which my dignity argument is based. There are pockets of scrounger culture in which living off welfare is taken for granted and, indeed, in which screwing the Social Security system with successful fraud can bring not shame but honor. I count myself extremely lucky not to have been born into such a culture, and am saddened by the breakdown in social cohesion that its spread represents. But I believe that a basic income would help to prevent that spread by giving citizenship a new meaning.

2. The reason there is a dignity-deprivation and social-exclusion problem is the strength of the work ethic. That is, having a job—making it clear to others that you are somebody who has some value in the labor market—is a precondition for first-class-citizen self-respect. And one's earned income (labor income) is seen, provided the activity that earns it is not criminal, as deserved—because it is a measure of the value which the market (always objective, of course, and therefore fair) places on your personal qualities.

Van Parijs talks of "work fetishism," and contrasts it with wanting everyone to have a job so that they can "find recognition and accomplishment." But the work ethic is about duty, not about seeking the positive rewards of recognition and accomplishment. It is about avoiding the charge of being a free-riding layabout. And it is for real. It is what makes our current welfare-to-work programs politically acceptable. And, for a basic income to have the most benign results, it would have to change. Decoupling work—having a job—from the status of citizenship is the first step. Tying the latter to something else—like doing some form of community service—might be the second.

Finally, for the belief that the market gives everyone their *just* rewards, we could reasonably substitute the notion that the clever, powerful, and influential, the captains of industry or the winners-taking-all, owe their highly enjoyable careers principally to the lucky deal they got in the genetic and family environment lotteries. If that were the general perception, it would surely not be on any "getting their just desserts" grounds that they could claim to enjoy higher incomes in addition to more power and admiration and job satisfaction, thanks to the intrinsic character of their jobs. Clearly the spread of some such social perception is a precondition for the level of redistribution through taxation that would be necessary to fund a large basic income.

Is such a revolution in social perceptions possible? How can one possibly guess? But we do know that income inequalities grow most rapidly in the societies with flexible labor markets, where income structures are less tied by convention and corporatist agreement and are more immediately responsive to supply and demand. And the market forces that lead to growing inequality are a consequence of the fact that as technology (social as well as material) gets more complex, the premium placed on the ability to learn to do difficult jobs grows, and jobs that almost anybody can learn to do become relatively scarce. Eventually, even in societies with less flexible labor markets, technology is likely to cause pretax income inequalities to grow and grow, however improbably successful the efforts to improve schools.

Growing income inequality means more envy, a growth of social exclusion, and a rise in antisocial subcultures. If antipoverty measures are all means-tested, this means a growth in benefit fraud—the estimated cost of which in Britain already produces some alarming figures. This will provide a growing argument for the abolition of means tests. And the growth of social exclusion, antisocial subcultures, at a time when the secular "decline in deference" is still in progress, means the growth of crime. "Sixteen percent increase in violent crime since last year," say the British headlines this morning. Middle-class fear of crime may prove the most potent argument for accepting the level of taxation necessary for a basic income. At that time, Van Parijs's arguments for the social justice of a basic income, together with a "luck, not deserving effort" perception of "success," might begin to have some bite.

WHY PAY BILL GATES?

FRED BLOCK

Philippe Van Parijs deserves our gratitude for seeking to stimulate a long overdue debate in the United States about the basic income concept. My disagreements with him are only tactical; they center on the problem of how to get the idea of a UBI taken seriously. Here, as elsewhere, Van Parijs struggles with the tension between his ideal vision of a UBI and a version of the UBI that would be politically and economically feasible. His procedure for resolving this tension is the weakest part of his argument.

In his ideal vision, receipt of the UBI is not conditioned by the individual's behavior, household status, or other sources of income, and the amount to be received is greater than a subsistence level. Behind this emphasis on unconditionality lies the intuition that people should be able to make their life plans, including how much they work and with whom they live, without anxiety about their ability to afford food and shelter. Secure in the knowledge that the UBI check will arrive every month, even the poor could escape endless worries about basic subsistence. I agree with this motivation for the UBI; the problem comes with implementation.

As Van Parijs quickly admits, this vision of a radically

unconditional UBI is very expensive. He acknowledges that
the increased taxes required to finance the net income transfers would be so disruptive that the UBI would have to be
phased in gradually. He doesn't address the related problem—the absurdity that even Bill Gates would receive his
monthly UBI check. Sure, wealthy people like Gates would
face higher rates of taxation that would more than offset the
UBI payment, but why bother cutting that completely un-
needed check?

Van Parijs's major strategy for resolving the issue of
expense is a gradual phase-in of the UBI payment. The
program would start well below the subsistence level and
be raised over a period of time. But he doesn't deal with
the potentially treacherous politics of gradualism. In the
United States, it is possible to imagine a scenario in which
a powerful insurgent movement wins the first stage of UBI
implementation after an extraordinary mobilization. Part
of the political deal launching this shift to unconditional
payments would involve the phasing out of a number of
means-tested and conditional payments. Yet what if, at the
second stage of implementation, opponents were politically
stronger and were able to block an increase in unconditional
payments while insisting on a continued reduction in older
transfer programs? The result could easily be that many
low-income households would be considerably worse off
than they were when the idea of a UBI was not taken seriously.

* * *

Given the difficulty of gradualism in highly polarized polities, the better path is to qualify the unconditionality of the grant. If the size of the grant is conditioned by level of income and household situation, the UBI becomes a negative income tax (NIT). As Van Parijs notes, the NIT provides a UBI in the form of a tax credit only to those individuals and households who qualify by virtue of insufficient income. Since NIT payments are so closely targeted to those who have inadequate levels of income, such a program is far more affordable and could be implemented in one shot. Most importantly, the design of the NIT could be modified so that it would function quite similarly to Van Parijs's ideal.

NIT payments could be made to households or individuals on a monthly or even weekly basis, and individuals who suddenly lose income—either because they left a degrading job or a degrading relationship—could receive some emergency assistance immediately and get the maximum monthly check within two weeks of notifying the tax bureau. (Karl Widerquist has suggested that individuals could designate a primary bank account for payment and receipt of taxes and the government would provide something like automatic overdraft protection.) The more knotty problem is that low-income individuals might reach the end of the tax year and find themselves overdrawn on their government account. Especially for those living closest to subsistence, the need to pay back the government would reintroduce the economic coercion that the UBI is intended to eliminate.

But even with an unconditional grant, a private version of overdrawing would remain common; people will take loans to make ends meet and the need to repay those loans would force them to take unattractive jobs or even return to an abusive spouse. Still, Van Parijs is hardly alone if he is concerned that public debt might represent a greater threat to personal freedom than private debt; the image of Dickensian officials demanding that the government be repaid immediately can be scary. But this scenario is hardly inevitable. For one thing, the scope of the problem could be reduced by exempting the first three or four thousand dollars of earned income from any taxation. Hence, an individual might receive a six thousand dollar negative income tax payment if his earned income was anywhere between zero and $4,000. Only when his earned income exceeded $4,000 would the negative tax credit be reduced. This would make the overall program more expensive, but it would substantially reduce the incidence of tax officials trying to extract back taxes from those living close to the margin. Furthermore, the rules could be written so that these low-income overdrawn individuals would have several years to repay with only nominal interest charges. Finally, there would also be a role for private charity. With the NIT in place, there would be less need for charitable efforts to provide people in need with food, clothing, and shelter. Charities could shift to making long-term investments in poor individuals and families, including low-interest loans for a variety of purposes, including repayment of both public and private debts.

In short, with a little creativity, the NIT design could achieve the ambitious goals for a UBI with the huge advantage that its initial implementation would immediately make virtually all the poor better off. Furthermore, supporters of a full scale NIT could quite reasonably argue that this represents a logical next step after years of successful experience in the United States with a NIT-like program—the Earned Income Tax Credit—that has been restricted to the working poor. Van Parijs is absolutely correct—misguided worries about making life too comfortable for the undeserving poor must not deter us from pursuing a reform with the potential to protect millions of people from the horrendous consequences of growing economic inequality.

SOMETHING FOR NOTHING?

ROBERT E. GOODIN

There are many reasons for preferring a "universal basic income" to the present pattern of social supports. Some are moral, others pragmatic. The pragmatics may be philosophically less showy, but they might also be politically more powerful. Here I shall supplement Philippe Van Parijs's useful roundup by offering another pragmatic reason for shifting to a universal basic income, and then suggest how that proposal might be politically saleable, even in seemingly hostile environments.

THE DESTANDARDIZATION OF SOCIAL LIFE

Public policymakers are long accustomed to responding to social need "categorically." Public assistance is offered under headings that supposedly correspond to the standard sorts of "social risks" that can characteristically lead to hardship: old age, sickness or injury, death or desertion of the household's breadwinner, unemployment, and so on. Those same categories also incidentally separate the "deserving poor" from the "undeserving," those whose hardships are ostensibly due to their own recklessness or fecklessness—but I'll leave that to one side for now. My present concern is with the limits of categoricalism, not as a form of social moralism, but as an instrument of social policy.[1]

Categorical approaches to the relief of social distress work fine only so long as people's lives and needs follow broadly predictable patterns. In late-Victorian England, Rowntree and Booth found that they did. The traditional sort of poverty that they uncovered basically tracked the life cycle: people were poor when they were young, when their own families were young, and again when they became too old to work.[2] With industrialization came other sorts of standard social misfortunes associated with the production process (occupational sickness and injury) and the economic cycle (unemployment).

Where social risks were relatively standard across the population, so too could be the social response. Governments instituted categorical benefits of one sort or another (child benefit, family allowances, old-age pensions) to address standard risks of poverty at various points in the life cycle. Governments mandated contributory social insurance schemes of one sort or another (unemployment, disability, old age, death, or desertion) to deal with cases in which industrial workers and their families were without market income. Social safety nets were still required to catch anyone whose needs were in some way peculiar, and not covered by any of those standard schemes. But those were supposed to be, and largely were, residual: small-scale mopping-up exercises, with the vast majority of cases being covered by one of those other standard programs of social relief.

In that world of "standard problems and standardized responses," public programs were propped up by other equally standard, nonpublic "pillars of social security." Assuming standard family relations (one partner for life) and standard employment relations (full-time, full-year employment with the same employer for life), people could ordinarily draw on family resources and occupational benefits to tide them over. That made them more "self-reliant," which in the context of this debate meant merely less reliant upon state support.[3]

That is "the world we have lost." Maybe it was never completely true anywhere. But certainly it is not true now for most people in most places in the advanced economies. The standard employment relation is no more. Most of us, we are told, ought to expect to have two or three careers across the course of our lives—and probably just as many partners (and fractured families). And that means that we can no longer rely on either of those nonstate pillars of social security. It also makes it much harder for public programs to process more than a few claimants through any small set of standard social categories. If people's needs are increasingly nonstandardized, so too must be the social response.

One way of doing that is to give more discretion to social workers and rely on them to be attuned to each person's unique circumstances. But that of course would represent a return to the old poor laws. It would remake welfare-right claimants into abject supplicants for the substantially discretionary favors of public and private charity.

To my mind, a much more attractive response to the destandardization of social life would be to abandon conditionality and categoricalism altogether. Let's give up trying to second-guess how people are going to lead their lives and crafting categorical responses to the problems they might encounter. Instead, simply give them the money and let them get on with it.

PARTICIPATION-CONDITIONED INCOME

That is an admittedly pragmatic argument for universal basic income. But the main arguments against universal basic income are essentially pragmatic as well. Philippe Van Parijs has effectively addressed the main economic ripostes encountered by such proposals. But an even more telling argument against universal basic income is political: whatever the abstract merits of the case, you will simply never be able to sell people politically on the idea that people should get "something for nothing," when everyone else in the community is working for a living.[4] Maybe, as Van Parijs says, surfers should be fed, but there is little political support for feeding them *so* well as to keep up the physically demanding sport of surfing at public expense.

This point is pragmatic in the first instance, principled in

{ 93 }

the second. There is no political constituency precisely because it offends people's principles (their sense of fair play) that someone should get something for nothing when others have to work hard for it. To some extent those principles are internalized by welfare recipients themselves, whose self-esteem is heightened if they are able to "give back something to society" rather than just being seen, by themselves as much as anyone else, as leeches on the commonweal. Whether or not those sentiments are well grounded, they are indisputably real and politically powerful. And that makes it politically impossible to enact a basic income in any universal and unconditional form.

Thus the most politically saleable form of basic income, for now and the foreseeable future, may be a "participation income."[5] Under that scheme, everyone would draw a basic income *on condition* that they perform some socially useful labor. They can satisfy that condition by working in the paid labor market. But equally well, they can satisfy it by caring for young, old, or disabled members of the community, by participating in community service or environmental projects, or through some other activity.

Obviously, participation income is conditional in a way that universal basic income is not. Equally obviously, everything depends on what counts as "socially useful labor" and who gets to decide whether any given person has done enough. At its worst, such a scheme could be as oppressive as the most tyrannical labor exchange. At its best, it could well allow people credit (and cash) for doing all sorts of good things that they want to do and perhaps would be doing anyway. In any case, participation income is pragmatically as close as many of us suppose we will ever be able to get, politically, to universal basic income.

In the present political climate, how can even participation income be enacted?

Start by recalling that some of the most progressive developments have come under the most unlikely regimes. Bismarck was a deeply conservative politician who nonetheless gave us the welfare state in its modern form. Nixon was a deeply ambiguous politician who came close to giving us a negative income tax.

Consider, more specifically, the history of the enormously generous Dutch "social minimum." Roughly speaking, that program pays money to any family whose income falls below half the median national wage—money enough to get them above that threshold, which is roughly what cross-national researchers would deem the "poverty line."[6] One might imagine that that program was the brainchild of left-wing politicians. But, as it happens, the social minimum was the bequest of a series of traditionally conservative "confessional" coalitions in the 1960s. Not only were its instigators conservatives; the arguments they gave were couched in traditionalist terms. They wanted, above all else, to give social recognition to the important unpaid contributions made by stay-at-home wives and mothers in the traditional social order.

Might the same sorts of conservative impulses that led to this Dutch "backing into progressive social policies" be marshaled in support of basic income in its participation-tested form? Recall, first, that certain sorts of social benefits have been participation-tested for years. From their earliest days, unemployment benefit programs have always contained requirements that recipients be "actively looking for work." Advocates of many of the more reactionary forms of welfare reform have recently urged, with considerable success, that that principle be extended. "Workfare" (or "active labor market policy" or "mutual obligation") requirements have thus been imposed on a wide range of social assistance.

Here's the twist. Suppose workfare requirements are taken to imply an "activity test" that can be satisfied in any of many ways. Central among them are, of course, activities directly related to paid labor markets: working in paid labor, looking for such work, training for such work. But also invariably included—either as exemptions from the "activity test" or as ways of satisfying it—are provisions for those who are themselves unable to work (by reason of age or disability) and provisions for those who are unable to work because of their responsibilities caring for young children. Those provisions, in turn, are increasingly expanded to include caring for not only pre-school-aged children but also disabled relatives. Those, in turn, are expanded to include provision for "voluntary" (which is to say, unpaid) participation in approved community-service or environmental-protection projects.[7]

At the end of the day, we may well find punitive and dra-conian workfare schemes being thereby transformed, in effect, into state salaries for socially useful labor of many (if not quite all) forms. Maybe unpaid labor in households without very young or disabled members might not be in-cluded. But all manner of other community work, which had previously been unpaid, might suddenly attract, in effect, a salary from the state.

All we then have to do is persuade people to apply for it. That is to say, we just have to persuade them that "the dole" is not just for people who find themselves out of paid work, but also for people doing socially useful unpaid work. Once that gestalt shift is effected, workfare will have become a first approximation to a participation income. Once again we truly will have backed into progressive social policy.

A DEBATE WE NEED

KATHERINE MCFATE

Philippe Van Parijs argues that his basic income proposal could raise issues of social justice and "inspire modest immediate reforms." Those who in the past have attempted to highlight the advantages of more universal European social policies for U.S. audiences will be justifiably skeptical. The last two rounds of federal welfare reform have moved in exactly the opposite direction, and a number of public opinion polls show strong support for work-based welfare, among low-income people as well as middle-class voters. For decades, U.S. policymakers have been obsessed with ferreting out the "undeserving" poor and promoting work.

Nonetheless, structural conditions in the United States may be setting the stage for a serious debate about basic income. The deregulation of labor protections and the erosion of traditional social programs have left larger numbers of people more economically vulnerable in the United States than in Europe, thus broadening the potential impact and appeal of a basic income approach. The question is will progressive forces in the United States rally behind a *proactive* radical innovation in social policy?

Liberals in the United States have spent an inordinate amount of time and effort trying to improve a sixty-year-old income support system that was born, during the New Deal, through compromises that left regionalism, racism, and entrenched local economic interests intact. Why treat as sacrosanct an income support system that legitimizes huge state and local differences in the treatment of poor families?

Because it could be worse. It could be better, too, but it never will be if income support debates continue to be choke-chained to a public assistance program designed for an economy and social institutions that no longer exist.

We need an income support system that reflects and supports the needs of workers in the current economy—an economy in which almost 30 percent of workers are in "nonstandard" employment. Most of these workers (and many others) do not qualify for pension coverage or unemployment compensation. (Almost two-thirds of Americans without jobs do not receive income assistance during periods of unemployment.) In many large cities, street corner day-labor pools are back in force because no income-support system for childless, non-elderly adults exists. A guaranteed basic income could create a social floor for all workers, particularly those in nonstandard, "flexible," low-skilled employment.

A guaranteed basic income could provide an income cushion to encourage periodic "re-skilling." As product cycles shorten and new technologies demand new and different skill sets, politicians and employers have encour-

aged American workers to acquire new skills and knowledge. But only a tiny proportion of workers in selected in-
dustries and occupations are provided with transitional
income assistance when they temporarily leave full-time
work to retrain or receive further education. Such investments are viewed as an individual's responsibility. Yet even
employers might support a basic income system that en-
couraged easier entry into and exit from work, and facili-
tated part-time work and training.

A well-designed basic income support system could reflect and support the diversity of American families and
provide parents with more options. Two parallel public policy debates about families, work, and child welfare are oc-
curring today, independently of one another. In one debate,
it is argued that poor children are better off if their mothers
are employed in paid work outside the home, while someone
else looks after the children. (The mothers are modeling the
work ethic.) In the second, it is argued that nonpoor children will be better off if their mothers forgo income (and careers) to become full-time caregivers. (The mothers are
demonstrating that their primary commitment is to their
children's welfare.)

In the first debate, the government will pay anyone but
Mom to provide child care; in the second, the government
provides a special child-care tax credit to encourage or induce Mom to stay home. A guaranteed minimum income
could neatly marry these two discussions: a working mother
could reduce her work hours, and a stay-at-home parent

would receive an independent source of cash assistance. It would highlight the time-versus-money trade-off that all families face and would privilege no one family type.

The United States desperately needs a public discussion that challenges the prevailing belief that a person's worth and social contribution can and should be measured primarily (or exclusively) by his or her income from paid work. The right kind of basic income debate could force us to examine the activities and behavior we value as members of a family, a community, and a democracy—as distinct from the activities that the market values.

For a growing number of Americans, the promise of permanent jobs that provide middle-class security has vanished. Work-based benefits are contracting. Yet our social policies are pushing larger numbers of people into more complete dependence on waged work. It's time to imagine a new social policy better suited to the exigencies of a post-industrial, global economy. Basic income as a mechanism of distributive justice? It's an idea worthy of public debate.

THE BIG PICTURE

PETER EDELMAN

Philippe Van Parijs makes a good intellectual case for his proposition. As he says, the idea is not new. But it has been some time since anyone proposed it, so it is interesting that it is surfacing again. One consequence of the so-called "welfare reform" in the United States is a modest resurgence of discussion of how to help people who have no cash income. This is good, because the issue now has particularly pressing significance. On any given day there are about one million women, plus their two million children, who have been pushed off the welfare rolls or can't get on welfare now, and have neither a job nor cash assistance. Restoring a cash safety net is urgent.

The UBI is one relevant idea. Others include a refundable tax credit for caregiving, which would provide income for people caring for children or for elderly or disabled family members. These ideas are a long way from being enacted, but the fact that they are being put forward is valuable.

To be honest, though, I am ambivalent about spending time just now on proposals like the UBI. If discussing a guaranteed income helps move the issue of income adequacy toward the front burner, I am pleased. Frankly, I am not sure that it does. At the moment, anyway, those who advocate an income guarantee in a way that is not directly related to work face a steep burden of persuasion. We *should* have a family allowance, or some kind of income base, in the United States. But I worry that serious pursuit of such proposals at the present time imposes an opportunity cost— the time not spent on more politically salient ideas that could actually be enacted, with immediate consequences for the lives of low-income people.

At best the UBI is only a piece of the picture, anyway. We actually have a UBI "cousin" in the United States—food stamps. It's not pure because it has some work requirements, but these are not stringently applied, so food stamps amount to an income guarantee of about $3,500 for a family of four with no cash income. They constitute an enormously important policy, but that policy is grossly insufficient if it is not nested in a mixture of other policies and strategies. In the "good old days," when "welfare reform" meant a guaranteed income, I used to worry that its adherents weren't concerned enough about policies to help people find work. I am still concerned that people on the progressive side who want to reduce poverty in the United States do not have a broad enough view, and I think the reappearance of ideas focusing heavily on cash income skews the debate and moves us away from that synthesis. Recreating a decent safety net for those who are not in a position to work is vital, but I would focus centrally on work, including attention to wages and working conditions, and treat proposals like the UBI more as a component than as a centerpiece.

* * *

I once had a conversation with Robert Kennedy, while he was running for president in 1968, that has stayed with me. I told him the staff was proposing to put his support for a guaranteed income in a position paper we were drafting on welfare. He said, "I'm not for a guaranteed income. I'm for a guaranteed job." His point was one of emphasis, because he did in fact favor provision of decent cash assistance for people who were not in a position to work. But he believed that we had excluded large numbers of people, especially young people of color, from the labor market, and he wanted to focus on remedying that awful set of facts. I have the same reaction to ideas like the UBI when we don't discuss them in proper context.

Experience with the 1996 welfare law has revealed three stories that need to be addressed in the forthcoming debate over its reauthorization. One is of those who have jobs but have not escaped poverty. The 60 percent of former welfare recipients employed on any given day are earning an average of about seven dollars per hour and working an average of around thirty hours per week. They need help with income, continuing health and child care coverage, and housing— and these are needs they share with millions of others who were never on welfare and are not, given the stingy way we define poverty, even considered "poor." A second story is of those who are off the rolls and not working. For those people, a safety net must be reinvented. In the short run this is only going to occur within the framework of the welfare structure created in 1996—not in talk about something like the UBI. The third story is of those still on welfare who are going to hit the time limits soon. Some of them, anyway, can work, but need a lot more help than they have gotten so far, and maybe a publicly supported jobs program as well. (And that's just the jobs and income side of the equation. We also need to invest in education and activities for children, attend to the special challenge of neighborhoods where poor people live in concentration, and reestablish in our inner cities the safe and supportive community environment the rest of us take for granted.)

So, while I appreciate Van Parijs's contribution, I don't think it gets us very far in the real world of policy and politics where the decisions will actually be made.

ON LIBERTY

GAR ALPEROVITZ

For several decades there has been a major hole in traditional theories of the structural requirements of liberty. Filling this hole is important in its own right; doing so also offers a powerful way for progressives to begin to challenge conservatives on what has historically been their high ground.

Conservatives have commonly argued that the principles of liberty are necessarily linked to capitalism as a system—especially entrepreneurial capitalism. They argue that the institution of individual entrepreneurship helps to disperse power away from the state; that it offers individuals a "place to stand," a certain independence of choice and action; and that it sustains a culture of independence rather than servility.

The notion that real freedom requires the economic independence that comes with the ownership of property was largely taken for granted among the Founding Fathers. Thomas Jefferson held that dependence "begets subservience and venality, suffocates the germ of virtue, and prepares fit tools for the designees of ambition." For John Adams, too, "equal liberty" required enabling "every member of society" to acquire land "so that the multitude may be possessed of small estates."

Throughout most of nineteenth- and much of twentieth-century America, the entrepreneur (often a small businessman or farmer-capitalist) continued to play a major role in the economy, and the close link between freedom and property-ownership can be found in a wide range of nineteenth century theories of the structural requirements of liberty. In the early twentieth century, Louis Brandeis (along with many others) doubted that "any man [could] be really free who is constantly in danger of becoming dependent for mere subsistence upon somebody and something else."

For at least a century, however, the entrepreneur has been displaced as the central factor in the political economy. The most perceptive conservatives recognized long ago that this displacement presents a fundamental challenge to their theories. Joseph Schumpeter, for instance, famously judged that capitalism would die if entrepreneurial property became marginal in the system: "The perfectly bureaucratized giant industrial unit not only ousts the small or medium-sized firm and 'expropriates' its owners, but in the end it also ousts the entrepreneur and expropriates the bourgeoisie as a class, which in the process stands to lose not only its income but also what is infinitely more important, its function."[1] With the decline of the entrepreneur in the corporate economy, the traditional structural basis of liberty itself substantially disappeared.

* * *

But if the institution of widespread entrepreneurial capital no longer provides for real dispersion of power, an individual place to stand, and a culture of independence, what then?

Some theorists—for, instance, Peter Drucker—have focused on the job, suggesting that guaranteed employment could be substituted for entrepreneurial property: jobs are (and should be) "becoming a nexus of rights and a species of property."

An even more powerful argument is that a guarantee of income (and we might add, of free *time*) provides a new foundation for liberty. The late Louis Kelso, a maverick conservative, endorsed this view, as does Philippe Van Parijs. But this focus, important as it is, is still somewhat narrow: apart from Van Parijs's secondary poverty-related, feminist, and green arguments, the main concern is with providing the individual with structural support for what might be called "real opportunity of choice." The broader arguments suggesting that an absolute guarantee of income is a necessary long-term, system-wide institutional basis for liberty—that an unconditional guarantee, built into the basic organization of the political economy, provides an essential basis for independence—intersect with and complement this argument, but they also transcend it. Academics understand the central issue rather easily in their own world when they defend tenure on this ground: liberty to speak out depends on a *guarantee* that one's means of livelihood will not be undermined.

Currently the U.S. economy produces approximately $130,000 for every family of four; by 2100 this number will grow, on conservative estimates, at least four-fold. It is reasonable to begin discussing a long-term trajectory in the direction of providing an unconditional guarantee of at least some portion of income as one way to begin to build a new system-wide institutional basis for liberty. (To be sure, transitional possibilities—understood as transitional, and as political compromises—will likely include various forms of work or other requirements.)

A limitation of Van Parijs's work (and that of most others writing on these matters) concerns how resources are gathered and allocated to achieve the various income guarantees. Van Parijs assumes the framework of a traditional social-democratic welfare state; he assumes in particular that sufficient political power can be mobilized by progressive groups to use the power to tax in order to pay for a basic income. With the decline of organized labor, and of other traditional sources of progressive power throughout the western world, this hope is fading.

In this connection, it is striking to note that Van Parijs highlights the model of the Alaska Permanent Fund, which in 1999 allocated almost $1,800 per year to each state resident (roughly $7,000 to a family of four). Alaska Fund income does not depend upon taxation but upon directly capturing returns from the public ownership of capital.[2] Experiments of this kind—and the theoretical work of writers like Kelso on the one hand, and John Roemer on the other—suggest a need to focus less on the tax-and-transfer system, and more on various forms of public democratization of capital. Over the coming century such a focus is likely to become a necessary condition of income-related strategies—and, ultimately, of a new structural basis for liberty capable of filling the gap in traditional approaches.

PATHWAYS FROM HERE

CLAUS OFFE

I agree with Philippe Van Parijs that a Universal Basic Income (UBI) is a morally attractive arrangement, and think he provides a normatively compelling argument for it in terms of real freedom and social justice. But I also believe that it is a mark of a good theory to be able to offer a theory about itself. In this second-order component, the theorist must answer, among others, the question: why do so many people oppose my theory? Why isn't it universally shared, given its overwhelmingly evident plausibility? Shared, that is, by a sufficient number of people, both elites and non-elites, to implement its prescriptions.

One answer to this question might be provided by an ad hoc list of propositions: people need to get used to the idea; they have to overcome their moral prejudices and intuitions; they are misled by interested parties into believing that the social costs of a UBI will be unbearable and that the benefits are dubious. These observations are obviously well taken. They suggest some strategies for improving the chances for a UBI to be successful: try to convince people, talk to political elites, demonstrate that the idea has fallen on fertile ground already in some countries, do more realistic econometric analysis on all kinds of second-order consequences, design and conduct large-scale experiments, and the like. All of this is actually being done, and with considerable success, most prominently by Van Parijs himself and also by other people involved in the Basic Income European Network (BIEN), various national research institutes, advocacy groups, and some left-libertarian political parties.

But while interest in and openness toward UBI schemes are generally on the rise, and not only so in the advanced economies, nobody would seriously claim that the reality of Basic Income (in the demanding version specified by Van Parijs) is just around the corner anywhere. Why not? I want to suggest an answer and derive a few (second-order) policy implications for proponents of the UBI idea.

As Van Parijs has argued, the ultimate justification for UBI is freedom: the freedom of individuals to say "no" to employers and state agencies (to say nothing about spouses) without being punished through material deprivation. As a general rule, the anticipation of freedom causes fear. As is the case with other instances of achieving freedom, this fear, although it can be passionate and exaggerated, need not be outright paranoiac. It can be based upon reasons. So, who has which reasons to fear what from the freedom that would follow on UBI? In numerous debates and confrontations I have had on the desirability and feasibility of Basic Income, I have encountered various kinds of fear.

1. Employers fear that their control over workers will be weakened, as workers would have a livable withdrawal op-

tion. A UBI makes it more difficult for employers to recruit workers for "bad" jobs, and requires employers to increase wages if they still want to fill these jobs.

2. Employees fear that a UBI will require a rate of (direct or indirect) taxation that in turn will involve a downward compression of the scale of net income; similarly, the UBI, they fear, will serve as a pretext to replace the wage-graduated "social wage" that employees receive as pensioners, or, in the case of unemployment, with a flat-rate transfer. Wage differences will thus no longer, or not to the extent they are used to, translate into differences in income transfers, and the relative loss of income will have to be made up for through savings.

3. Prospective UBI recipients fear that the level of their income, including the rate of increase of their income, will be contingent upon political decisions and fiscal constraints, and thus be determined in the future by majorities who may or may not endorse and remain faithful to the idea of economic citizenship rights.

4. A great variety of individual and corporate actors fear for the moral underpinnings of a social order that is no longer shaped by the "productivist" assumptions that (employed or self-employed, at any rate market-rewarded) work is "normal," free lunches "anomalous," and the demand of "something for nothing" deviant.

It seems to me that proponents of UBI must take these fears seriously. To suggest otherwise would be to ignore the deep traces that more than one hundred years of the hegemony of industrial capitalism have imprinted upon ideas, intuitions, and expectations. In fact, these hegemonic forces have forged an inter-class alliance founded on a work-centered normative belief system that appears to be largely immune to revision, even under the impact of the manifest changes of social and economic realities. Numerous and prominent policy intellectuals advocating "welfare-to-work" schemes believe—or at any rate espouse the belief and encourage people to adopt it—that the *only* device by which modern societies can both integrate individuals *and* at the same time grant them a measure of autonomy is the labor contract. Although we can no longer ensure every adult a permanent job that pays a decent wage, this empirically obsolete vision of "normality" is more firmly entrenched than ever at the normative level. Proponents of a UBI have been rightly disgusted by this perversity, but they have yet to find a way of coping with it in politically productive ways.

So what might be done? I suggest that efforts to implement a UBI should be governed by principles of *gradualism* and *reversibility*. The idea is to provide a context in which people can change their preferences through learning, as in the saying that the appetite comes with the eating (rather than with coercive feeding). Instead of thinking about the UBI in terms of "before" and "after," we need to conceptualize and promote it in the dynamic terms of less and more. This intellectual and political mode of experimental approximation could move along the following pathways.

As is well known, in an eventual steady state of a fully implemented UBI even the "surfer" or the "bohemian" would be entitled to a subsistence level citizen (or even resident) income—a scandalous anomaly by today's prevailing standards that proponents of UBI are usually quick to mitigate by speculating that nobody is likely to adopt the idle life of a surfer for any length of time. But another strategy of response is possible. Note that in most advanced economies and their social policy systems, numerous types of people in various situations and activities are effectively entitled to tax-financed income transfers, at a subsistence level or even higher. Single parents of infants belong in this category, as do people performing mandatory military service. The same applies to families, university students, and—within the European Union and as long as the Common Agricultural Policy lasts—farmers. Institutionalized exemptions from market labor (or the exclusive reliance of market rewards for labor) are numerous and perfectly legitimate.

One gradualist strategy, then, would be to expand the list of groups, conditions, and activities that are legally eligible for such exemption. Political initiatives to promote such expansion are all the more promising as the "third" or "voluntary" or "self-help" sector of private foundations, cooperatives, and neighborhood organizations begins to play an increasingly visible role both as a social phenomenon and as a policy device to unburden, as well as increase the effectiveness of, state-provided services. To be sure, such "participation income" (as Tony Atkinson has influentially termed it) is still not "unconditional," but rather contingent on non-market services performed. But the more popular, normal, and widespread the sector of such voluntary activities becomes, the more effectively can the authoritarianism of external bureaucratic control be fought.

As is equally well known, a fully implemented UBI would eventually reach subsistence level (and preferably also both legislative irreversibility and continuous adjustment to current market income); it would also be free of any means testing; and it would be effectively paid to all citizens and residents. But these three features constitute as many axes of gradual approximation. More specifically, one could think of starting with an income supplement that does not cover the subsistence level but would still open up a withdrawal option in terms of hours of work. One could make means-testing less stringent and also invert the means-test from one measuring lack of means to one measuring the presence of (significant) assets, with the implication being that all citizens *except* those with assets above a specified level receive a basic income.

In his presentation here, Van Parijs does not mention that the UBI is not just universal, unconditional, and subsistence-covering, but also permanent. It is individually paid from adolescence to the end of life. The temporal extension is a further dimension of gradual approximation, and indeed an especially promising one. Elsewhere I have argued for a "sabbatical account" (of, say, ten years) to which every adult person is entitled and upon which she can draw at any time (after the age of, say, twenty-five) in the form of chunks of time of at least six months, and use the free time, which is covered by a flat-rate income, for whatever purpose she chooses. This scheme can be understood as a temporary basic income. The freedom of choice as to when, as well as how much of it, to withdraw will help to reduce the labor supply at any given point in time. It will also allow employees to (threaten to) withdraw from particularly undesirable jobs and working conditions, and it will provide opportunities and incentives to restore skills and other aspects of human capital. Instead of "banning" people from the labor market, they are provided with the economically tolerable option of opting out voluntarily and temporarily, thus contributing to the restoration of "full" employment, if at a lower absolute level. Those making use of the option would also indirectly contribute to what I consider to be one of the most attractive feature of UBI (and most of its half-way approximation): the powerful indirect effect it would have upon what we used to call "work humanization" and the gradual elimination of particularly "bad" jobs.

In conclusion, and having in mind the context of the European Union and its integration, let me highlight one dimension in which gradualism is *not* feasible. A UBI (or whichever of its incomplete approximations) cannot be introduced in one country alone. For such unilateralism is likely to trigger migration effects that are bound to under-mine the political and economic viability of any even less-than-complete solution. (Such migration, or emigration-prevention effects are, of course, intended in the very special case of Alaska, as they were intended, before 1989, in the comparable case of West Berlin, with its residence premium paid to citizens as tax credit.) In Europe, however, what is possible in one country is constrained by what is possible in all other countries as well and at the same time. This rule may well be interpreted "Euro-skeptically," as proof that the European Union stands in the way of national policy inno-vation. But it may also be read, more optimistically, as a de-sign for the implementation of a "social" Europe that might be capable of providing some much-needed meaning and broad popular appeal to the project of European integra-tion.

3

REPLY

PHILIPPE VAN PARIJS

What an unexpectedly sympathetic set of comments! No doubt unrepresentative of U.S. public opinion. But it's a start. I will focus my comments here on the most critical remarks, concentrating first on issues of normative justification, then on questions of political strategy.

JUSTIFICATION

As Emma Rothschild and Brian Barry aptly recall, part of the case for a UBI appeals to efficiency and to the general interest. The crucial normative battle, however, is to be fought in terms of justice. I believe that justice requires that we maximize the minimum level of real freedom, and that a UBI is an especially compelling way to secure justice thus conceived. Elizabeth Anderson and William Galston reject my conception of justice in favor of a view based on reciprocity, and more specifically on the obligation of the able to help the needy—the traditional moral basis of welfare-state programs. To achieve the objectives flowing from this conception, Galston finds a combination of targeted programs more effective than a UBI that provides income for everyone. Anderson, who is particularly sensitive to the stigmatizing and exclusionary impact of targeted programs, is more cautious: empirical evidence may show that a UBI is part of the best feasible package. Precisely this sort of evidence on social and economic trends has turned Robert Goodin and Katherine McFate into advocates of a UBI, on the basis of a normative conception that does not seem that different from Galston's and Anderson's. A harder look at these trends—for example, Goodin's idea that risks are now less standardized—should turn the critics, too, into somewhat reluctant, pragmatic advocates of a modest UBI.[1] In short, the case for UBI does not depend on embracing the real-freedom theory of justice.

Toward the end of her comment, however, Anderson hints at a totally different normative foundation of social transfers, one which offers the promise of a more direct justification of a UBI. The Alaska case, she notes, "suggests that the legitimation problem in the United States could be solved by funding the UBI through revenues collected on the use of public property." The underlying normative insight is illuminatingly developed in Herbert Simon's and Ronald Dore's comments. In Simon's formulation, it consists in "recognizing shared ownership of a significant fraction of the resources, physical and intellectual, that enable the society to produce what it produces." From this view, it does not follow, as Gar Alperovitz suggests, that the legitimate funding of a basic income can only take the form of dividends on public assets. Some taxes, such as the pollution or energy taxes advocated by Anne Alstott and Barry, can easily be interpreted along these lines. More fundamentally, as explained by Simon and Dore, even taxes on labor income must be understood not as the confiscation of part of the fruit of a worker's effort, but as a fee on the use of lucky opportunities by relatively high-paid workers.

This key insight takes us from a traditional conception of the welfare state as a combination of (self-interested) insurance and (more or less generous) solidarity, to one that also includes an idea advanced by Tom Paine: that there is a set of transfers to which one is entitled neither by virtue of one's contributions nor one's neediness, but simply by virtue of one's membership in the relevant community. No need to restrict this claim, as Paine did, to natural resources, nor to base it, as Paine did and Barry suggests one must, on alleged "natural rights." We need only recognize the moral arbitrariness of (very unequally distributed) opportunities in order to see that whatever we are given is—as regards distributive justice—"public property."

Elsewhere, I have tried to elaborate this view systematically into a conception of the fair distribution of real freedom that also pays due attention to the special needs of the handicapped, to the importance many people attach—in Europe no less than the United States—to social recognition through paid work, and to the moral ugliness of deliberately living at other people's expense.[2] To be sure, this view is the target of many philosophical objections. Given the constraints of space, I cannot respond those objections here, but instead refer interested readers to my replies to two recent collections of critical essays.[3]

STRATEGY

"One could starve to death talking about income independent of wages," says Wade Rathke. Along the same lines, Peter Edelman notes that pushing for a UBI may involve a hefty opportunity-cost in terms of "time not spent on more politically salient ideas that could actually be enacted." I agree. Even those who are convinced that a UBI is part of what we should aim at must agree that there are contexts in which, and people for whom, it does not make sense devoting much time and energy thinking about it, let alone mobilizing for it. There are many important problems a UBI would not fix, and many important problems more attainable measures could fix.

Nonetheless, even in the seemingly most hopeless situations, it is part of some people's job to keep exploring and advocating the politically impossible. First, as Barry emphasizes, seismic events do occur, and it is important to prepare intellectually for when a political opportunity suddenly arises. Second, if a carriage is stuck in the mud and you want to get it moving in the right direction, the best policy is rarely to make everyone scrape under the wheels or push at the back. Some people should pull ropes quite some distance ahead, while others investigate alternative routes much further afield.

An essential part of the forward-looking thinking that is required consists of working out the best transition strategy, which may vary greatly from one country to another.[4] In one place, family policy may be the best point of departure (McFate), in another the development of sabbatical accounts (Claus Offe). Even existing workfare schemes may prompt a move towards a UBI through a gradual broadening of the work condition in response to the difficulty of providing suitable standard jobs for all claimants (Goodin). This process could lead to a "participation income"—a UBI subjected to the performance of some (paid or unpaid) socially useful activity. Goodin, Offe, and Barry believe that imposing such a condition would considerably increase the political chances of a UBI, in Europe no less than in the United States. So do I, while also believing, along with Barry, that a rigid participation income scheme risks opening up "a nightmarish scenario of an enormous bureaucracy entrusted with arbitrary monitoring powers," which will either lead to regression or, as we both hope, to an unconditional basic income.

In the U.S. context, however, the best basis from which to build is probably the Earned Income Tax Credit. Ronald Dore and Fred Block emphasize the potential for turning it into a negative income tax (NIT), which Block regards as "far more affordable" and therefore politically more realistic than a UBI. For a given level of income guarantee, an NIT is not more affordable than a UBI in an economically relevant sense. It only looks more affordable because of a frequent failure to perceive the economic equivalence between benefits and tax expenditures.[5] The variant sketched by Block is even less affordable, in this sense, than a UBI financed by a flat tax on all income, because of the exemption it proposes on the first $3,000 of earnings. Yet, I agree that using the NIT route is politically most promising, both in Europe and the United States, when income tax is used as the main source of funding. This is not, however, a matter of true economic cost, but of fiscal cosmetics.

Those who think that EITC needs to be reshaped in the direction of an NIT or a UBI believe, along with Alstott, that it does not give people enough room for reducing working time or taking a break. Others, like Edmund Phelps, believe that the EITC gives people too much of it, and that it must accordingly be reformed in the direction of hourly wage subsidies channeled through the employers and restricted to full-time workers. Phelps sees no reason to "feel sorry about women 'subjected to the dictates of a boss for forty hours a week.'" On the contrary, this gives them "a sense of contributing something to the country's collective project, which is business."

I have no authority to speak about America's collective project, but I would find it sad if it were reduced to business, and terrible if someone managed to convince those women that their dignity, their pride, the meaning of their lives were to be found in full-time submission to a boss. Along with Alstott, I believe instead that it is a great advantage of a UBI that "it comes without strings, so that women can choose for themselves how to spend the cash" and that it "places that choice squarely where it belongs—with women." Empowering the weakest, spreading the "independence" emphasized by Rothschild and Alperovitz to those currently dependent on bosses, husbands, or welfare officers, are to me no less worthy objectives than business. According to Adam Smith (*pace* Rothschild), pursuing them may not even be bad for business. And even if it were, it would remain an imperative for the sake of liberty and justice for all.

Hard and bold thinking about UBI and the means to achieve it is essential for those committed to this less degenerated interpretation of America's collective project. There is no reason to believe that they cannot win. But they will do so only if they do not let themselves be intimidated by a concern for "relevance" in today's climate. Only if they dare to speak out.

NOTES

Van Parijs / *A Basic Income for All*

1. Many academics and activists who share this view have joined the Basic Income European Network (BIEN). Founded in 1986, BIEN held its eighth congress in Berlin in October 2000. It publishes an electronic newsletter (bien@etes.ucl.ac.be), and maintains a web site that carries a comprehensive annotated bibliography in all EU languages (http://www.etes.ucl.ac.be/BIEN/bien.html). For a recent set of relevant European essays, see Loek Groot and Robert Jan van der Veen, eds., *Basic Income on the Agenda: Policy Objectives and Political Chances* (Amsterdam: Amsterdam University Press, 2000).

2. Federal senator for the huge state of Sao Paulo and member of the opposition Workers Party (PT), Suplicy has advocated an ambitious guaranteed minimum income scheme, a version of which was approved by Brazil's Senate in 1991.

3. Two North American UBI networks were set up earlier this year: the United States Basic Income Guarantee Network, c/o Dr. Karl Widerquist, The Jerome Levy Economics Institute of Bard College, Annandale-on-Hudson, NY 12504–5000, USA (http://www.usbig.net); and Basic Income/Canada, c/o Prof. Sally Lerner, Department of Environment and Resource Studies, University of Waterloo, Waterloo, Ontario, Canada N2L 3G1 (http://www.fes.uwaterloo.ca/Research/FW).

4. See James Tobin, Joseph A. Pechman, and Peter M. Mieszkowski, "Is a Negative Income Tax Practical?" *Yale Law Journal* 77 (1967): 1–27. See also a recent conversation with Tobin in BIEN's newsletter ("James Tobin, the Demogrant and the Future of U.S. Social Policy," in *Basic Income* 29 [Spring 1998], available on BIEN's web site).

5. See Joseph Charlier, *Solution du problème social ou constitution hu-*

manitaire (Bruxelles: Chez tous les libraires du Royaume, 1848); John Stuart Mill, *Principles of Political Economy,* 2nd ed. [1849] (New York: Augustus Kelley, 1987).

6. See the exchange between Eduardo Suplicy and Milton Friedman in *Basic Income* 34 (June 2000).

7. The latest countries to introduce a guaranteed minimum income at national level were France (in 1988) and Portugal (in 1997). Out of the European Union's fifteen member states, only Italy and Greece have no such scheme.

8. In the United States, one recent proposal of this type has been made in Fred Block and Jeff Manza, "Could We End Poverty in a Post-industrial Society? The Case for a Progressive Negative Income Tax," *Politics and Society* 25 (December 1997): 473–511.

9. Bruce Ackerman and Anne Alstott, *The Stakeholder Society* (New Haven: Yale University Press, 1999). Their proposal is a sophisticated and updated version of a proposal made by Thomas Paine to the French Directoire. See "Agrarian Justice" [1796], in *The Life and Major Writings of Thomas Paine,* P. F. Foner, ed. (Secaucus, N.J.: Citadel Press, 1974), pp. 605–23. A similar program was proposed, independently, by the New England liberal, and later arch-conservative, Orestes Brownson in the *Boston Quarterly Review* of October 1840. If the American people are committed to the principle of "equal chances," he argued, then they should make sure that each person receives, on maturity, an equal share of the "general inheritance."

10. For a more detailed discussion, see Philippe Van Parijs, *Real Freedom for All* (New York: Oxford University Press, 1995).

11. One can think of alternative normative foundations. For example, under some empirical assumptions a UBI is also arguably part of the package that Rawls's difference principle would justify. See, for example, Walter Schaller, "Rawls, the Difference Principle, and Economic Inequality," in *Pacific Philosophical Quarterly* 79 (1998): 368–91; and Philippe Van Parijs, "Difference Principles," in *The Cambridge Companion to John Rawls,* Samuel Freeman, ed. (Cambridge: Cambridge University Press, forthcoming). Alternatively, one might view a UBI as a partial embodiment of the Marxian principle of distribution according to needs. See Robert J. van der Veen and Philippe Van Parijs, "A Capitalist Road to Communism," *Theory and Society* 15 (1986): 635–55.

12. See Edmund S. Phelps, *Rewarding Work* (Cambridge, Mass.: Harvard University Press, 1997).

13. In the U.S. case, for example, the fiscally equivalent negative-income-tax scheme proposed by Block and Manza, which would raise all base incomes to at least 90 percent of the poverty line (and those of poor families well above that), would, in mid-1990s dollars, cost about $60 billion annually.

14. To fund this net cost, the personal income tax is obviously not the only possible source. In some European proposals, at least part of the funding comes from ecological, energy, or land taxes; from a tax on value; from non-inflationary money creation; or possibly even from Tobin taxes on international financial transactions (although it is generally recognized that the funding of a basic income in rich countries would not exactly be a priority in the allocation of whatever revenues may be collected from this source). But none of these sources could realistically enable us to dispense with personal income taxation as the basic source of funding. Nor do they avoid generating a net cost in terms of real disposable income for some households, and thereby raising an issue of "affordability."

15. Along the same lines, Herbert A. Simon observes that "any causal analysis explaining why American GDP is about $25,000 per capita would show that at least $^2/_3$ is due to the happy accident that the income recipient was born in the U.S." He adds, "I am not so naive as to believe that my 70% tax [required to fund a UBI of $8,000 p.a. with a flat tax] is politically viable in the United States at present, but looking toward the future, it is none too soon to find answers to the arguments of those who think they have a solid moral right to retain all the wealth they 'earn.'" See Simon's letter to the organizers of BIEN's seventh congress in *Basic Income* 28 (Spring 1998).

EMMA ROTHSCHILD / *Security and Laissez-faire*

1. *Réflexions sur le commerce des blés* [1776], in *Oeuvres de Condorcet*, ed. A. Condorcet, O'Connor, and M. F. Arago (Paris: Firmin Didot, 1847–1849), p. 111.

2. John Stuart Mill, *Principles of Political Economy with Some of Their*

Applications to Social Philosophy [1848], in Mill, *Collected Works,* vol. 3 (Toronto: University of Toronto Press, 1965), p. 962.

3. F. A. Hayek, *The Road to Serfdom* [1944] (London: Routledge and Kegan Paul, 1971), pp. 89–90.

4. Adam Smith, *An Inquiry into the Nature and Causes of the Wealth of Nations,* ed. R. H. Campbell and A. S. Skinner (Oxford: Clarendon Press, 1976), p. 610.

5. Hayek was concerned about these difficulties in his account of minimum income policies in 1944. See *The Road to Serfdom,* p. 90.

EDMUND S. PHELPS / *Subsidize Wages*

1. In conversation and correspondence I could never get him to endorse this interpretation. But he never protested it either. In a 1985 letter he commented that the presentation of his system on pp. 144–49 of my textbook *Political Economy: An Introductory Text* (New York: W. W. Norton, 1985) accurately presented his position. That exposition makes explicit the premise that society is a cooperative enterprise for the contributors' mutual gain.

2. Some argue that this flow is the largest that can be legitimately redistributed. Aspects of the matter are taken up in Robert Nozick, *Anarchy, State, Utopia* (New York: Basic Books, 1974).

3. Europeans call the underground the "informal" economy and see as it as a charming zone of idyllic exchange rather than a parasitic sector that lives off the legitimate economy through tax evasion and other covert practices that subvert respect for the law.

BRIAN BARRY / *UBI and the Work Ethic*

1. Keith Bradsher, "G.M. Has High Hopes for Vehicle Truly Meant for Road Warriors," *New York Times,* August 6, 2000.

2. Stuart White, "Review Article: Social Rights and the Social Contract—Political Theory and the New Welfare Politics," *British Journal of Political Science* 30 (2000): 507–32. I can heartily recommend this article, incidentally, for a discussion of a number of the issues surrounding basic

NOTES

income and its rivals. For "participation income" see Tony Atkinson, "The Case for Participation Income," *Political Quarterly* 67 (1996): 67–70.

ELIZABETH ANDERSON / *Optional Freedoms*

1. In defense of this thesis, see my "What is the Point of Equality?" *Ethics* 109 (1999): 287–337.

2. Amartya Sen has consistently made this point in opposition to egalitarian views that regard resources as the relevant space of equality. See, for example, *Inequality Reexamined* (Cambridge, Mass.: Harvard University Press, 1992).

ANNE L. ALSTOTT / *Good for Women*

1. Bruce Ackerman and Anne Alstott, *The Stakeholder Society* (New Haven: Yale University Press, 1999). Ackerman and I propose that high-school dropouts should receive what is, in effect, a basic income. See pp. 37–39. We also propose a separate program of flat-rate citizens' pensions, which pay a basic income to the elderly. See pp. 129–54. We discuss why we favor stakeholding over a UBI at pp. 210–16.

2. For example, current Social Security provides for a spousal benefit and mandatory annuitization of benefits; both features tend to redistribute toward women. Some privatization plans would repeal both features.

3. Econometric studies routinely find that labor supply is not highly responsive to taxation. For recent research on this issue, see the papers collected in Joel Slemrod, ed., *Does Atlas Shrug?* (Princeton: Princeton University Press, 2000).

ROBERT E. GOODIN / *Something for Nothing?*

1. These points are elaborated in my "Crumbling Pillars: Social Security Futures," *Political Quarterly* 71 (2000): 144–50, which builds in turn on my "Toward a Minimally Presumptuous Social Welfare Policy," in *Arguing for Basic Income*, ed. Philippe Van Parijs (London: Verso, 1992), pp. 195–214.

2. B. Seebohm Rowntree, *Poverty: A Study of Town Life,* 2nd ed. (London: Macmillan, 1901); Charles Booth, *Pauperism and the Endowment of Old Age* (London: Macmillan, 1892).

3. I argue this point in "Social Welfare as a Collective Social Responsibility," in *Social Welfare and Individual Responsibility: For and Against,* David Schmidtz and Robert E. Goodin, eds. (New York: Cambridge University Press, 1998), pp. 97–194.

4. What finally did in Aid to Families with Dependent Children in the United States and cognate programs around the world was arguably increased female labor force participation. So long as the ordinary expectation was that women of school-aged children would stay at home with them if they were economically able, a case could be made for public assistance to allow other women to do so as well. But once middle-class mothers were typically "working for a living" in the paid labor market, "welfare mothers" were increasingly expected to do the same.

5. Such a proposal has been endorsed by the U.K. Labour Party's Commission on Social Justice. See *Social Justice: Strategies for National Renewal* (London: Random House/Vintage, 1994). Elaboration is provided by Tony Atkinson, a member of that commission, in his "The Case for a Participation Income," *Political Quarterly* 67 (1996): 67–70.

6. "Roughly," because exact payments depend on household structure, and so does the "poverty line"; but it is the flavor of the program rather than the details that matter here.

7. In Australia, for example, the unemployment benefit ("Newstart Allowance" or "Youth Allowance") is subject to a "mutual obligation" activity test which can be met through "voluntary work 24 hours each fortnight for at least 8 of 13 fortnights" for 18–20 year olds, or 30 hours for people over 21. The agency responsible for administering that scheme says, on its web page that "the choices of voluntary work are almost limitless: helping people with disabilities; helping people who are frail; home care; shopping; administration; community welfare; translating; providing companionship and support; working with community-based organisations or clubs." For further information, see http://www.centrelink.gov.au.

NOTES

GAR ALPEROVITZ / *On Liberty*

1. Joseph A. Schumpeter, *Capitalism, Socialism, and Democracy*, 3d ed. (New York: Harper & Row, Publishers, 1950), p. 134.

2. Individuals receive payments from the Fund derived from the public investment of oil royalties in a wide range of assets. For further discussion of practical institutional models involving the public or quasi-public ownership of wealth, see my "Who Owns Capital?" *Boston Review* 24, 1 (February/March 1999): 40–42.

PHILIPPE VAN PARIJS / *Reply*

1. Rawls's conception, which both Galston and Edmund Phelps invoke against UBI, is not as first-best-inimical to a UBI as the traditional social-democratic conception. See my "Difference Principles," in *The Cambridge Companion to John Rawls*, Samuel Freeman, ed. (New York: Cambridge University Press, 2001).

2. See Philippe Van Parijs, *Real Freedom for All* (New York: Oxford University Press, 1995).

3. See "Basic Income? A Symposium on Van Parijs," *Analyse und Kritik* 22 (2000); *Real Libertarianism Reassessed: Essays on Van Parijs* (London: MacMillan, forthcoming).

4. There is certainly no need to wait for a global UBI to be feasible before introducing it in any particular country. The migration problems mentioned by Galston, Rothschild, and Barry can be handled in the same way as they are under existing means-tested schemes.

5. See section 3 of Philippe Van Parijs, "Basic Income: A Simple and Powerful Idea for the XXIst Century." Background paper for BIEN's eighth congress, Berlin, October 2000, available from http://www.etes .ucl.ac.be/BIEN/bien.html.

ABOUT THE CONTRIBUTORS

GAR ALPEROVITZ is author of *The Decision to Use the Atomic Bomb* and (with Jeff Faux) *Rebuilding America*.

ANNE L. ALSTOTT is professor of law at Yale Law School. She is the co-author (with Bruce Ackerman) of *The Stakeholder Society*.

ELIZABETH ANDERSON is professor of philosophy, women's studies, and law at the University of Michigan. She is author of *Value in Ethics and Economics*.

BRIAN BARRY is Arnold A. Saltzman Professor in Philosophy and Political Science at Columbia University. He is author, most recently, of *Culture and Equality*.

FRED BLOCK teaches sociology at the University of California—Davis.

JOSHUA COHEN is professor of philosophy and Sloan Professor of Political Science at the Massachusetts Institute of Technology. He is editor-in-chief of *Boston Review* and author of numerous books and articles in political theory.

RONALD DORE'S latest book is *Stock Market Capitalism, Welfare Capitalism*.

PETER EDELMAN is professor of law at Georgetown University Law Center.

WILLIAM A. GALSTON is director of the Institute for Philosophy and Public Policy at the University of Maryland, College Park. He is author of *Liberal Purposes*.

ROBERT E. GOODIN is professor of social and political theory and philosophy at the Research School of Social Sciences at the Australian National University in Canberra.

KATHERINE MCFATE is a program officer at the Rockefeller Foundation.

CLAUS OFFE is professor of political science at Humbolt University in Berlin.

ABOUT THE CONTRIBUTORS

EDMUND S. PHELPS is McVikar Professor of Political Economy at Columbia University. He is author of *Rewarding Work: How to Restore Participation to Free Enterprise*.

WADE RATHKE has been chief organizer of ACORN for the past thirty years.

JOEL ROGERS is professor of law, political science, and sociology at the University of Wisconsin; a member of the *Boston Review* editorial board; and author of numerous articles and books on American politics.

EMMA ROTHSCHILD directs the Centre for History and Economics at King's College, Cambridge, England. Her new book, *Economic Sentiments*, will be published next year.

HERBERT A. SIMON is University Professor of Psychology and Computer Science at Carnegie Mellon University. In 1978, he received the Nobel Prize in Economic Sciences.

ROBERT M. SOLOW is Institute Professor of Economics, Emeritus, at the Massachusetts Institute of Technology. He won the Nobel Prize in Economics in 1987, and is author of numerous books and articles on economic growth, labor markets, and macroeconomics.

PHILIPPE VAN PARIJS directs the Hoover Chair of Economic and Social Ethics at the Catholic University of Louvain, France. He is author of *Marxism Recycled* and *Real Freedom for All*.